First edition: 2025
© 2025. Arturo Gómez Quijano (Coordinator).
Ediciones Universidad de Navarra, S.A. (EUNSA) University Campus • University of Navarre • 31009 Pamplona • Spain
+34 948 25 68 50• www.eunsa.es •eunsa@eunsa.es

ISBN: 978-84-313-4053-7
DL NA 1351-2025

Cover and editorial design: Malinche Studio SL
Printed by Podiprint
Printed in Spain

Aristotelling!

The art of persuasive communication

Arturo Gómez Quijano (Coordinator)

CONTENT.

PROLOGUE

Neither arguments nor emotions are decisive: what really counts is the credibility of the speaker.

Aristotle

PROLOGUE

Athens, late fourth century B.C. A city state where everything –from a trial to the election of a government position to promotions in the army– was decided by popular vote, after listening to the speeches of the various speakers. It was the right context for the birth of a new profession: those who helped public speeches get votes. Their business proposal could be summarized as: **"Tell me which cause you want to defend, and I'll help you win."**

These "mercenaries of the word" offered their rhetorical services at the best price. A good speech starter, a sequence that works, a story that moves, evocative poetry, a rhyme that makes the message more memorable... and even a funny nickname to ridicule the adversary.

Before them, Aristotle from Stagira stood up to defend another model of what today we would call leadership. In the Areopagus, surrounded by his fellow citizens, he raised his voice to proclaim: "Neither arguments nor emotions are decisive: what really counts is the credibility of the speaker. Therefore, not every cause can be defended, but only an idea in which the speaker is a legitimate defender."

The Stagirite labeled these paid rhetoricians the derogatory adjective "sophists," experts in using fallacious arguments ("sophisms") to persuade others. For Aristotle, "Persuasion is the quality that allows the speaker, through his credibility, his emotional connection and his arguments and proofs, to convince his audience of a point of view or a behavior, because it's beneficial for both of them."

Twenty-five centuries have passed since then, but nothing has changed. Today, as it was then, there is a proliferation of those who teach public speaking as if it were a technique without soul. As if persuasion and manipulation were almost the same thing.

In the book you hold in your hands, we defend the opposite: persuasive skills are an important part of good leadership, characterized by a mentality of service to those who listen to you. A good leader does not "rule", imposing his vision using the strength from his job title, money or fear, but persuades (the "'soft power'") so that people follow his recommendations freely. A skill that has its point of strength in ethics, which is the root of credibility.

Surely, in these pages you will find structures that work, useful tips on how to create a good message, and recommendations on verbal and body language. These tips come from the accumulated experience of the authors, all expert trainers of managers. We recommend them because they work, but they are not magic recipes. They work because they are rooted in an anthropological vision of the human being. Aristotle was certainly a great rhetorician, but above all, he was a great philosopher.

In fact, the authors of every chapter –top level professionals– each with their own style, follow a method they have developed over time, with their own likes and preferences. But in this essential work we have agreed to appeal to the common principles of rhetoric as developed by Aristotle in an organic way.

We hope that it will be helpful to any reader, but we recognize we have set it up with participants in the executive programs of IESE in mind, the management school of the University of Navarra, where we teach Communication Skills courses. It is a book made by many hands, by those who have written them and by others, as there was not enough room for everyone. It is the collective work of the team that has been training professionals for many years to become better leaders by making better decisions, which always have an ingredient of communication.

This is not meant to be an academic publication (there are great books on this, some of them signed by members of the team) but to offer a short summary of the essentials, to be used to prepare the exercises in our courses and to return to when in professional life we have to make a proposal to the management committee, a few words in a difficult negotiation, a lecture on a tricky challenge, or simply a nice story to celebrate a professional achievement or to say goodbye to a loved person.

We are sure that these words of advice will help you, whether you are already doing it very well or are still far from excellence. The most important thing is that you never give up or become satisfied. Remember that public speaking is not a theoretical matter. It is like riding a bicycle: there is always some theory, but above all there is personal effort, a determination to improve with every speech, and practice, practice, practice.

So, if I may give you some advice, follow the recommendations below, but don't forget the main thing. Some of the magnificent daggers made in Toledo were engraved with the legend: *Don't trust me if you lack heart.* Good communication comes from within, it is not a disguise but a way of being and leading.

Dr. Yago de la Cierva

After graduating in Law from the University of Santiago de Compostela and a PhD in Philosophy from the University of Navarra, he has worked as a journalist (founder and CEO of the News Agency ROME Reports TV), director of corporate communications and professor at several Business and Communication Schools in seven countries. He also provides Crisis Management consultancy for companies and non-profit organizations.

After teaching at IESE for many years, in courses related to corporate communication, crisis management, media relations, public affairs and reputation, ESG risk management and public speaking, in the MBA, MIM, executive education and tailor-made programs, Yago de la Cierva is now the President of Universidad Villanueva Foundation.

Communication.
Some basic
concepts

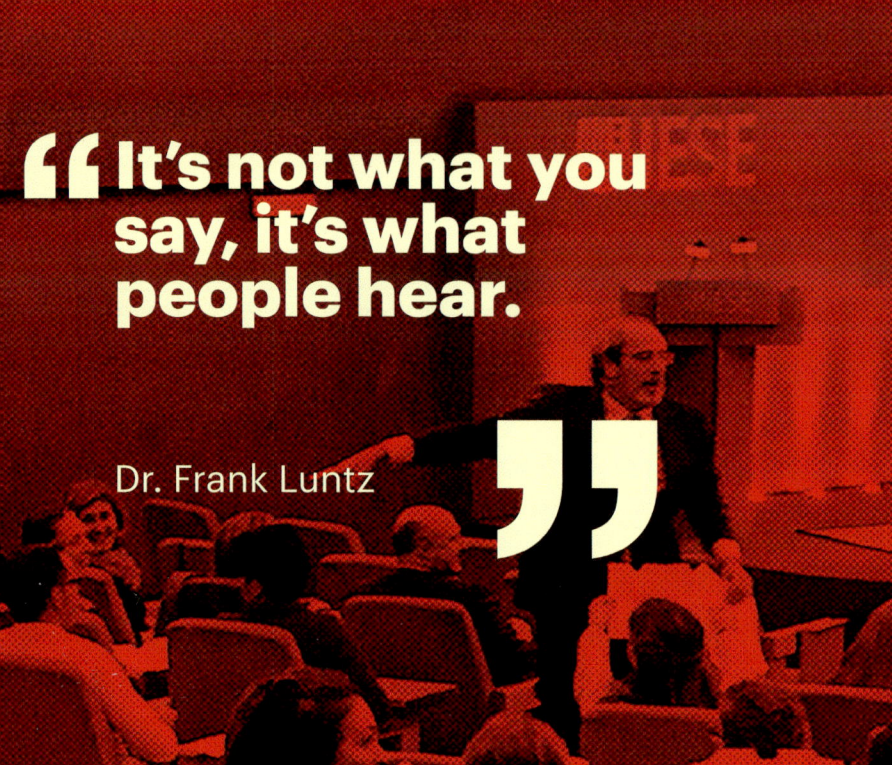

"It's not what you say, it's what people hear.

Dr. Frank Luntz

"

Communication is the other. The most important thing is not what I say, but what the other understands. When the audience changes, everything changes. It is essential to know the audience to communicate effectively.
IESE Business School, a meeting with professors from Institució Familiar d'Educació, Barcelona, November 10th, 2018.

Communication is the other

"We will not accept any more donations." Médecins Sans Frontières (MSF) made this surprising announcement only a week after the tsunami disaster that struck the Indian Ocean in December 2004. They already had all their programs properly funded for the emergency in the region. The response was that MSF received 110 million Euros, when 25 million Euros was the budget foreseen to finance all the projects for the following year[1].

People understood that MSF was the most credible organization to send their money for tsunami relief. Their announcement increased donations, even though they said they had already funded all their projects and would not accept any more funds. That statement helps us to understand the following: "It's not what you say, it's what people hear." This idea, taken from Frank Luntz[2], helps us to put the focus of our communication not on me, but on my audience. Moreover, in communication we deal with perceptions, rather than facts or data.

1 https://www.msf.org/sites/default/files/2018-06/msf_tsunami_operations_overview_one_year_on.pdf
2 Words That Work: *It's Not What You Say, It's What People Hear,* is the title of one of Dr. Frank Luntz's bestsellers, Grand Central Publishing, August 2008.

In this chapter you will learn the key concepts of effective communication: how to put the focus on the audience, the three steps of the communication process, the types of discourse and the art of storytelling, the most powerful tool of all.

Focused on the other, your communication should have three steps:

The key skill is listening

The communication starts with the other, when someone receives something. In persuasive communication we want our audience to do (or stop doing) something that we believe is good for them, and good for us. But this is not going to be so easy for you.

We will not be able to communicate effectively unless we know anything about our audience: Who are they? How many are they? Where are they from? Which language do they speak? What is their age or education? Without this information you will not be able to connect.

Knowing your audience is your first task. We call it: listening. Imagine you wanted to attract or make someone fall in love with you. How would you prepare your meeting with that person? What they need from you, what they care about you, what they would like from you. Think also about how he/she will see you (perceptions) and what he/she expects from you (expectations). Communicating is like falling in love: everything revolves around the other person.

In the book *The Art of Presenting*[3], the author proposes *"the map of the audience's needs."*

---

3 *El arte de presentar: Cómo planificar, estructurar, diseñar y exponer presentaciones (The Art of Presenting: How to plan, structure, design and deliver presentations)*, by Gonzalo Álvarez Marañón, Gestión 2000, May 2012.

These are nine questions that will help you better understand the audience you are addressing. Answer them to prepare your communication:

- How many are there?
- Who are they?
- Why are they here?
- What are their concerns?
- How can I solve their problem?
- What do I want them to do?
- How can I best engage them?
- How might they resist?
- What do they know about the issue?

Connecting on three levels

Once you know your audience, you can move on to the next step. This knowledge will help you to connect better. The connection with your audience should be made on three levels:

- *They must understand what you say (rational).*
- *You must engage them with what you say and how you say it (emotional).*
- *They must believe and trust what you tell them (credibility).*

Connect with the minds of your listeners so that they understand you better. Use images and concepts that help them understand what is new, by reference to what they already know. The message must be well explained and argued. You should reinforce the main idea you propose with other ideas. The example of Médecins Sans Frontières increasing their income by saying they could no longer accept donations explains the abstract idea that communication is not what you say but what the other person understands.

Put the thermometer on your audience to find out their emotional temperature: What emotions are present? What is the predominant one? How is the audience feeling at that moment? Imagine for a moment that you are addressing a very angry audience, and you don't know it. Could you connect with them? It would probably be difficult. I remember that, when I was young, I worked on a concert tour with a very well-known singer. The stage was my responsibility. He always asked me before going out, *"How's the audience?"* I became his *emotional thermometer*.

Ask yourself also what credibility you really have:

- *What authority do I have to speak to this audience?*
- *Why should they believe what I tell them?*
- *What would I have to give them to get them to do something?*

If you speak in front of someone, your credibility is always at risk. On the cover of the book by Frank Luntz that I quoted before, the first word that appears is "Dr.". Or is it by chance Frank Luntz the same as Dr. Frank Luntz when it comes to endorsing the content of a communication book? Is it irrelevant whether it says *"New York Times Bestseller"* on the cover? That book, and no other, is recommended by the most prestigious newspaper in the world; that book is the one most people have bought. Establish your credibility. Present your achievements. Get others to introduce you. Show your credentials to be there in front of the public. They will give you credit and back up everything you say.

Sharing: the last step that finalizes communication

If you have done the previous steps properly, then you will be able to achieve what you are looking for.

Sharing is essential in communication; this is its purpose. If you want your communication to be effective, you must share something that really has value, not for you, but for your audience. Imagine someone tells you that he is going to show you a way to earn your first million euros. Wouldn't you pay attention to them?

Listening is the first step, which will let you know clearly what's relevant to your audience. The main question that should always guide your communication is:

- *What do I have that is relevant to my audience? What do I have of value that my audience appreciates?*

What I want to achieve with my communication

The most attractive part of the speech must be used to draw the attention; the relevant part to be effective. In an environment so saturated with empty messages, you will succeed if your message is attractive and relevant to your audience. But you should ask yourself what change you want to provoke in your audience:

- *In their knowledge: What do I want them to* **KNOW?**
- *In their perception: What do I want them to* **FEEL?**
- *In their behavior: What do I want them to* **DO?**

If you want people to know something, you will have to give them data, figures, facts. Is this all you really want them to know? If you want your audience to feel something, you will have to share your emotions, attributes, values... How do you want to make them feel? If you want your audience to do or not do something, you will have to give them incentives to do it. What will they gain if they do what you say?

The languages of communication

"I'm going to kill you!" As you well know, communication cannot be only verbal. If you only use verbal language your communication will be incomplete and therefore ineffective. Think of a text-only message on WhatsApp: "Don't do this to me again, I'm going to kill you!" In Spanish culture this could be a loving message from someone who has forgiven us for an important mistake.

But in other cultures, the message could be received as very aggressive and violent text. We need to know the tone, the context. We need to see the other person's face to understand it better. If you saw a slight smile on his/her face, the message could be understood differently.

Ask yourself:

- **What I say** (the words you are using, **the verbal** language)
- **How I say it** (the context of what you are saying, **the paraverbal** language)
- **What I do** (your behavior, which is also a message, **non-verbal** language)

We receive the message through all three channels and, almost certainly, the one that contains the most information is the non-verbal one. When we relate to others, our behavior has the value of a message. This is what leads Paul Watzlawick[4] to affirm that "it is not possible not to communicate." Think for a moment that you are always communicating, even if you don't say a word. The absence of behavior is also a message.

YouTube tutorials are a clear example of the effectiveness of the use of all languages in the same communication. My 85-year-old mother uses them when she is not sure how to make a recipe. My 23-year-old son uses them when he doesn't understand how to install software. We can go to them to understand something better, because they explain it (verbal) and, in addition, you can see how it is done (non-verbal). Remember: to be effective, always use all the languages of communication.

The power of communication: unity

Once you have mastered the different languages, the next challenge is to align your message. If anything can make your communication more powerful, it is unity. But what is really unity?

Unity is achieved by doing three things:

- *Pick a single idea and find three arguments to support it **(Structure)**.*
- *Say the same idea everywhere, adapted to each environment **(Repetition)**.*

---

4 *It is not possible not to communicate,* by Paul Watzlawick, Herder Editorial, January 2014.

- *Try to have few differences between what you say and what you do (Coherence).*

In communication there is only space **for one idea.** One single idea. If there is more than one idea, it loses effectiveness. Imagine that, without warning, your teacher calls you to the blackboard and throws seven paper balls in the air and tells you to try to catch them all. Most likely, you will catch only one or none at all. If the teacher did this exercise with the rest of your classmates, the same thing would happen. But everyone would catch a different ball. On the other hand, if the teacher threw just one ball of paper at you, you would have a much better chance of catching it. Throwing a lot of ideas in a message is a guarantee of confusion.

Another quality that makes communication effective is **repetition.** How do we learn to speak? By repetition. And... a foreign language? By repetition. How do we learn to add, to multiply, to sing, to pray...? By repetition. Repetition is essential in communication. Notice that, in advertising, whether on television, radio, in the press, on social networks, they always repeat the same advert. It is about repeating the same idea, without changing it, but adapted to the characteristics of each of the media.

Finally, **coherence.** Imagine that, at the company Christmas dinner, you hear your boss saying, 'people are the greatest treasure of this organization'. However, that same boss makes your life miserable, treats you very badly at work for the remaining two hundred and twenty days of the year, which message do you get? Which of the two do you give more credibility to? Just that. Before addressing someone, think about whether your behavior towards that person is coherent, whether they are saying the same thing as what your words are going to say.

Be sure that it will take time and effort to find the powerful idea that you need for your communication. As there will also be other ideas, you will have to organize them:

- *Find a single main idea, of high value and interest to share with your audience (Relevance).*
- *Organize all the ideas. The main idea must be more important than the secondary ideas you use to support it (Hierarchy).*

- *Bring the secondary ideas in line with the main idea, so that there is no doubt or contradiction between them **(Alignment).***

Three types of speech

Once you have clear that you must listen, connect and share, you are aware of the change you want to bring about in your audience, you know that you have three types of language, and that the unity of your communication is very important, you only have one question left to ask yourself:

- *How can you reach them better?*

Now it is time to think about which type of discourse is best suited to each situation:

- *If there are arguments that can support your proposal to convince the audience: use **rational discourse.***

- *If your experience and authority support the change you are asking your audience to make, prepare a **credibility speech.***

- *If the audience is gripped by an overriding emotion: you will need an **emotional speech.***

But remember that there really are no pure speeches. Most of the time you will use a combination of all three. My recommendation is that, depending on the circumstances, you must choose the dominant structure. If it is a rational speech, you will need to establish your credibility and you will need to connect emotionally with the audience. In the following chapters we will explain how to do this.

And a great tool: the art of storytelling

In any of these three types of discourse (rational, credibility, or emotional), you have the most powerful tool since human communication began: the art of storytelling. This instrument will help you, better than any other, to capture attention, to visualize your ideas, and to explain your messages.

But this manual is not just about teaching you techniques. We want to help you transform the way you communicate. With the help of exceptional experts who will share their experience with you. For your reflection. For you to find your own, personal, authentic style. For your action. So that you can make your communication a more effective tool that has a real and lasting impact and helps you to achieve the goals you set yourself.

Dr. Arturo Gómez Quijano

Lecturer and entrepreneur in communication, with more than 40 years of professional experience. PhD in Journalism and degree in Information Sciences from the Complutense University, PDD from IESE Business School.

He currently teaches undergraduate and postgraduate courses at Universidad Complutense de Madrid, IESE Business School, ESIC Business & Marketing School, ICEX- Universidad Internacional Menéndez Pelayo, Universidad del Sagrado Corazón de Puerto Rico, and Colegio de Estudios Superiores de Administración (CESA) in Colombia.

He has written 7 books and 7 cases on communication, business, and professional development. He has trained professionals in Spain and in 16 other countries.

02.

The message.
The power in communication

"How well we communicate is determined not by how well we say things, but by how well we are understood.

A Way to Learn · A World to Change

Andrew Grove **"**

The power of the message in communication

When we talk about communication, we usually focus on form: the tone of voice, body language, words. Although these elements are certainly important, **the message** is essential. It is the core that gives meaning to everything else: not just what we say, but the intention behind it.

The form matters, of course –it has been shown that non-verbal language transmits more than words– but what is crucial is that all elements must be consistent with the message. Without that consistency, confusion or mistrust arises. Think of someone who talks about the importance of smiling with a frown.

What impact does it have?

Before preparing a speech, it is essential to ask oneself: what message do I really want to transmit? And even more: **why is it important**

to the listener? If the message does not connect with the interests of the audience, it loses force, no matter how logical or well formulated it may be.

Once we have the answer to this question, we are ready to prepare our message. And to do so, we cannot forget that the secret of any good speech is a clear and direct message.

In short, a message is effective when it is clear, direct, inspiring, coherent and relevant. It is in this connection between what the sender wants to say and what the receiver needs to hear that true communication is born.

To help you in this process, we have created a four-step guide to build impactful presentations and get your message across clearly and powerfully to the audience.

4 keys to a speech that connects

01 KNOW YOUR AUDIENCE:
Before speaking, listen, find out who they are, what they are interested in, what concerns them.

02 CHOOSE THE RIGHT ARGUMENTS
What you say should matter to them, use data, stories or examples that speak directly to them.

03 IDENTIFY THE PROBLEM AND SET OUT THE OBJECTIVE
What problem are you going to solve? Clarify what conflict, doubt or need you are going to address.

04 CREATE AN IMPACTFUL SPEECH
Structure + rhythm + language Capture attention from the beginning and keep interest until the end.

Source: Claudio Hernández Olalla

1. Know your audience: the first step in effective communication

As mentioned in the previous chapter of this book, in any communication, the most important thing is not what we say, but to whom we say it.

We will not go into depth on this point for that reason, but to summarize, it is important to be clear that a well-structured speech loses impact if it is not aligned with those who are listening to it. Therefore, the real starting point is to know the audience.

Adapting speech not only improves its effectiveness, it also humanizes communication. Reminds us that we don't speak for ourselves, but to make a real impact on those who listen. And when the message connects with the audience, words reach their true power.

2. Chose the right arguments: the art of speaking to the people who listen

Once we understand who our audience is, the next fundamental step in the preparation of any speech or presentation is the selection of the arguments. It is not only a question of choosing the ideas that we consider most important, but of identifying those that will have the greatest resonance and impact on the people in front of us.

We know that not everyone processes information the same way. What convinces some, leaves others indifferent. Therefore, one of the secrets of persuasive communication is knowing how to adapt arguments to the cognitive and emotional profile of the audience.

According to how they tend to value the information they receive, in general terms, we can distinguish three main types of audience:

* **Data-oriented people:**

    This type of audience needs objective and verifiable evidence. They value numbers, studies, graphs, statistics and everything that brings rigor and objectivity to the message. For them, assertions without empirical support lack force. They are not easily convinced by inspiring phrases, but by concrete facts.

- **Experience-oriented people:**

  These people are more impressed by real examples, personal stories, anecdotes that illustrate a concrete situation. They value what they have experienced, what they can visualize or imagine. A well-narrated testimony can have, for them, more weight than a table of data. Empathy, in this case, is a powerful tool.

- **Authority-oriented people:**

  This group gives credibility to arguments that come from expert voices or recognized institutions. When an assertion is supported by a reference figure, a prestigious entity or someone with moral or technical authority, it acquires greater validity. Citing a Nobel Prize winner, a respected leader or an official organization can make a difference.

In practice, most audiences combine these three profiles to different degrees. Therefore, the most effective is to construct a message that integrates different types of evidence: a well-chosen figure, a moving story and a reliable source can work together to reinforce the impact of the speech.

The key is to observe, listen and adapt. If you are speaking to a technical team, you will probably have to rely more on data and evidence.

If you are addressing an educational community or a group of volunteers, the emotional and experiential may carry more weight. If the context requires institutional support, reference to authority will be essential.

Choosing the right arguments is not only a question of content, but also of communication strategy. It is a gesture of respect for the audience and a sign of the speaker's emotional intelligence.

Because when you speak in the language that the other person understands, when you take the time to think about how your interlocutor thinks, your words are not only heard: they are understood, appreciated and, in the best case, remembered.

3. Identify the problem and define the objective: give direction and purpose to the speech

Public speaking is not simply passing on information. It is, above all, an act of transformation. A good speech is not limited to presenting ideas: it seeks to provoke change, awaken awareness, generate reflection or drive action. You need to be oriented to do this. You must respond clearly to three fundamental questions:

A. What problem does the audience have?

B. What solution are you proposing as a speaker?

C. What action do you expect your audience to take?

These questions not only provide structure and clarity to the message but also give it meaning. When a speech starts from a real necessity –even if it has not yet been named by the audience– and moves towards a concrete solution, the connection is immediate.

The message is no longer abstract and becomes something useful, relevant and transformative.

A. Identify the problem

Many times, the audience feels a certain discomfort but has not verbalized it. The effective speaker knows how to put that discomfort, need or contradiction into words. Naming the problem accurately generates a connection: *"That's just what's happening to me."*

B. Propose a solution

After describing the problem, it is time to offer a concrete answer. It can be an idea, a tool or an approach, but it must be understandable, realistic and applicable. Vague solutions do not mobilize; clear ones do.

C. Invite to action

A good speech is not limited to reflection: it calls for action. Whether changing a belief or deciding, the action must be clear. That is the key to leaving a mark and transforming.

An effective speech must be a meaningful journey: it starts with a problem, offers a solution and leads to action. This structure guides both the speaker and the audience and gives strength and coherence to the whole message.

4. Keys to creating a powerful message: how to make your ideas make an impact

A truly effective speech is not limited to transmitting information. It goes beyond that: it must capture attention, generate interest, move emotions and, above all, remain in the memory of those who listen to it. To do this, the message needs more than solid content; it requires form, intention and a certain narrative sensitivity. In other words, what you say is not enough: how you say it really matters. We will discuss below some essential elements that transform the right message into an engaging one, capable of connecting with the audience and leaving a lasting impression:

- **Clarity:** The message should be summarized in a single sentence. If it is not understood quickly, it will not be remembered. Speak clearly is an act of generosity.

- **Accuracy:** *The less the better.* Remove the unnecessary and speak with precision shows respect for the audience's attention.

- **Simple language:** Profound ideas can be expressed in simple words. Plain straight talk is not simplifying but communicating well.

- **Stories:** Stories connect, humanize and are remembered. They are the best channel for bringing ideas to life.

- **Visualization:** Activating the imagination with images, metaphors or visual resources helps to anchor the message.

- **Emotion:** What excites it is remembered. Talking from sincerity generates proximity and connection.
- **Surprise:** The unexpected generates interest. A provocative phrase or narrative twist can make all the difference.
- **Motivation:** The message should answer "what's in it for me?". If it adds value, it will have an impact.

One of the differentiating elements that make the message memorable and impactful on the audience deserves special mention: ***soundbites.***

A *soundbite* is a short, precise and memorable phrase that summarizes a key idea and offers the audience a guide to remember the most essential, even when the details are not clear.

It's like a flash of clarity in the middle of a speech, a spark that grabs attention and stays in the memory, especially useful when the audience has disconnected. It doesn't need to be brilliant or fancy: Just need to say a lot in very few words.

Here you have some examples of soundbites. As you can see, although as a rule soundbites are brief, not seldom are they seen at greater length, but equally impactful and memorable:

- *"Being clear is not optional, it is essential."*
- *"Do not ask yourself what your country can do for you, ask yourself what you can do for your country."* J.F. Kennedy.
- *"A well told story is worth a well told hundred facts."*
- *"No one is born hating another person because of the color of their skin, their background or their religion. People learn to hate. They can also be taught to love."* Nelson Mandela.

A powerful message does not arise by chance. It is the result of intention, listening and care in every word. Because when we speak with clarity, emotion and purpose, our ideas are not only understood, but they are also felt, remembered and, very often, transformed into action.

Conclusion: the footprint of a good speech

Communicating well is not just talking well. It's understanding, connecting, make sense and leave a mark. Along these keys we have gone through the essential pillars of a speech that really impacts: know the audience, choose the right arguments, identify the problem and define the objective, and build a clear, relevant and memorable message.

Every step is an invitation to go beyond the surface, to speak with intention, to stop focusing only on the form to give prominence to what really matters: **the value of the message.**

When the communication is well planned, when the content is adapted to the listener and expressed with authenticity, including memorable soundbites, something powerful happens: the speech is no longer a monologue and becomes an act of gathering.

In summary, communicating with impact is not a question of talent but of preparation, empathy and purpose. And when a message comes out from there, it has the power to change not only what people think, but also what they do.

Reference material

Videos:

•   Harrison Ford on climate change:

https://www.youtube.com/watch?v=VAX7Qz8uO7A

•   Susan Cain on the power of introverts:

https://www.youtube.com/watch?v=cOKYU2jOTM4&list=PLNToFzk_WOHstp1tZxxL8TSxLkO_3_wW6&index=3&pp=iAQB

Example:

What story do you want your body to tell 10 years from now?

Maybe the story of someone who gave in to lack of time, stress, comfort? Or the story of someone who, despite everything, chose to take care of himself, chose to get stronger, chose to respect his life?

Because, after all, the body speaks. It speaks today. And it will speak even louder tomorrow.

Every day that passes without moving, every week that you decide to postpone it, your body feels it, even if you still do not notice it.

Until a day, without warning, appears in an injury, in a tiredness that won´t go away, in a disease that reminds you of what you didn't want to see.

And you know what's even more shocking? The surgeons, when open a body during an operation, they can tell in seconds if that person has ever played sports in his life. It's not magic. They see it in the quality of the muscles, in the resistance of the tissues, in the vitality of every cell.

An exercised body is like an imprint: it leaves written the commitment you had with yourself, even if you can no longer speak.

Exercising is not an additional cost, nor a caprice. It is not something "I'll do when I have more time".

Exercising is an act of respect. Respect for your health. Respect for your future. Respect for the people who love you and will want to see you strong and present for a long, long time.

It's not about training three hours a day. It's not about running marathons. It's something much simpler. It's about understanding that your body is your first project, your first business, your first home.

And if you don't take care of it, everything else sooner or later falls apart.

So today, when you finish listening to me, ask yourself again:

What story do I want my body to tell 10 years from now?

The good news is that you still have time to write it as you like.

Every session you sweat, every muscle you activate, every mile you walk or run, will be added up. Not to your appearance but to your life.

The difference between those who will be restricted tomorrow and those who will be free tomorrow... starts to be built today.

It is up to you!

But remember: **the body you take care of today... will be the one that saves you tomorrow.**

Claudio Hernández Olalla

After graduating in Business Administration from Universidad Pontificia Comillas in Madrid, Claudio began his career as a strategy and operations consultant (Deloitte and NTT Data).

He later joined ISS Spain, a multinational Facility Management company with 35,000 people in Spain, where he held various positions in both the commercial and operations departments. In 2022, he was appointed Head of Training and Development.

Claudio also works as a consultant, trainer and executive coach in his own company, Create Talent.

He graduated from the Executive MBA at IESE Business School in 2020, where he regularly collaborates as a professor of Communication in various programs. Claudio is certified as an executive coach by the International Coaching Federation (ICF ACC).

Logos.
The rational
discourse

"I have nothing to offer but blood and toil, tears and sweat."

Winston Churchill

Logos: The most solid temple for public speaking

The *logos* is the structure in which the speaker is least relevant. And, at the same time, it is essential that the speaker is very clear about what he or she wants to achieve with this speech.

The *logos* discourse is the rational discourse by essence, used to transmit knowledge. Not persuaded by emotion or rhetorical figures but by rational evidence.

In *logos,* the speaker's mission is to present evidence and propose a change to the audience. For the audience to make the decision to accept the proposal, the speaker provides the relevant data for the audience to decide. That is why we also call it "the expert's speech."

Hence, rational discourse works well when conclusive and reliable evidence is provided to support a proposal.

Structure of *logos*

The *logos* is like a Greek temple, which endures over time, through the centuries. Everything is arranged in a systematic and classical way. Its beauty lies in its proportions.

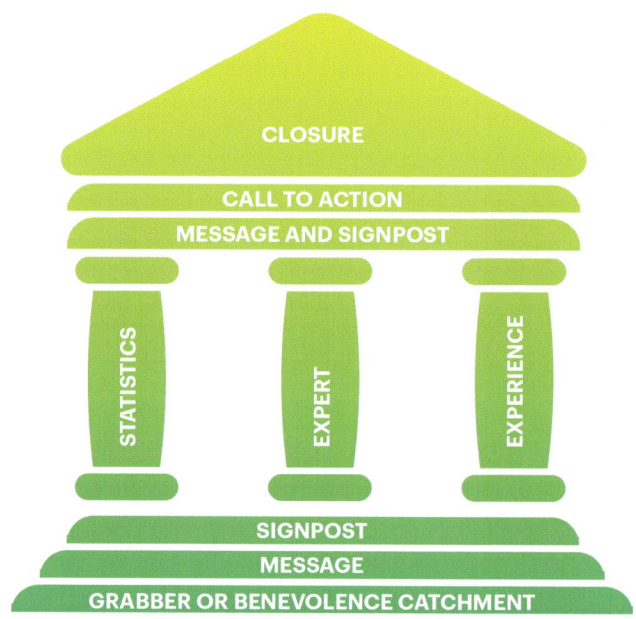

All speech can be compared to a human body: you have the bones or skeleton, the muscles and the skin. The bones constitute the structure. The mission of the skeleton is to give strength and proportion to the whole body.

And what is the skeleton of logos speech like?

1. Grabber or capture of benevolence

The speaker needs to grab the audience's attention and want to give them time to come up with a proposal. The "once upon a time", the beginning of any story, is broken down into four elements with which we introduce the audience to our story: time and place where it happens, common situation and complication that leaves the listeners hanging on a thread, or curious enough to ask us to continue.

Let me give you an example: "Three years ago I was in my office on the 24th floor of Torre Espacio. I was looking out of the window at the snow-capped mountains of Madrid, I felt quite satisfied. I had recently been appointed head of the finance department. Then the phone rang. It was my boss. – Carlos, come to my office. I immediately got up and went over. – I want you to present the annual accounts to the Board of Directors tomorrow because we need the budget to be increased. My vision blurred and the 24 floors seemed like an abyss. I had never been able to speak in public and now my boss was putting all his trust in me to convince that bunch of old geezers...".

What do you think? There are other ways to start a *logos* speech: with a rhetorical question that engages the audience, by sharing a fun fact with a suggestive quote from a person, but stories are usually the best option.

The basis of the discourse thus begun is solid enough to move on to the second point.

2. Message

The speaker pitches the main idea, a proposal he puts before his listeners. If the grabber requires attention, the message needs to be very comprehensible. Eight words. No more: subject, verb and predicate. It has to be brief. Concise. Clear. Direct.

An example: "Schools should teach public speaking".

Such a clear message cannot be interpreted in a different sense than the one you intend. Another thing is whether you have succeeded in convincing the audience about the message. That road begins now.

3. Signpost

The signpost (or marker) is said in five seconds but requires a few minutes of reflection. Public speaking is used to get the listener to change a perception or modify a behavioral pattern. In other words, to get them to move from point A to point B. And that is sometimes quite difficult. First you must convince them of the reasons and then you must motivate them so that they want to make the effort.

That is why the speaker, in preparing the speech, should investigate what benefits listeners will get from accepting his proposal. It's good to ask five, ten, twenty. And choose three. No more. The "triad" works well in oratory because anyone can remember.

It is often known that Winston Churchill convinced the British public of the need to become more involved in the Second World War with a speech in which he promised "blood, sweat and tears." Indeed, that was the case. However, what he stated was, *"I have nothing to offer but blood and toil, tears and sweat."* Four things, which history - or collective memory - has reduced to three.

At this point, the speaker must select three benefits and name each one with a single word. If possible, memorable, resonant, which contains a prize within it.

For example: "employment, security and internationalism".

Look, you haven't convinced anyone yet. In fact, some of them may be twisting their noses. That's why you need to share with them, as soon as possible, the weight of evidence.

4. The three columns of the temple

Here lies the key to the discourse of *logos*. The solidity of the Greek temple is supported by these three columns, the three evidence. Statistics, the Expert, and Experience.

Up to this point, the speaker must consider that part of the audience is skeptical about the intentions of the speaker. Therefore, the speaker will present compelling arguments. The speaker's task here is to select arguments that also offer a tangible benefit to the audience.

Because one thing is to be proven right, and another, different and more complicated, is to change their behavior. They will do so if it results in a gain for them. So, the three pieces of evidence must be three benefits.

The first one is addressed particularly to rational individuals. It involves presenting a statistic –quoting the data and the source– that supports the argument. Following with the example, the first sign-post might read: "According to a study from Harvard University, pub-lished in 2024, the ability to express oneself orally increases the like-lihood of securing employment by 85%."

As we mentioned earlier, part of the audience may not fully believe the speaker. The persuasive skill at this point consists of quoting a phrase from a highly authoritative expert that affirms what the speak-er intends to convey. "According to so-and-so - an expert from PISA[1] in the linguistic area, students who learn public speaking from the age of three develop an almost innate confidence to engage in com-plex environments."

Finally, it is usual that among the people who listen to us there are some *gregaries*. In other words, they act if they see that others have done so before and have benefited from it. For this reason, the third column is "experience." It consists in giving an example, own or ex-ternal, which confirms the veracity of our statement. For example, "the group of schools X adopted the oratory subject five years ago and have achieved remarkably excellent academic results in reading comprehension in the international tests of the International Bacca-laureate, which have facilitated their students' access to universities in other countries."

In this way, with the three pieces of evidence, the speaker has just convinced the audience that his message is valid, good, and rele-vant. Now, the most important thing is missing.

5. The message-signpost

As a general rule, the speaker devotes more time to the three pieces of evidence than to the other elements of the *logos*; now they must prepare the conclusion. They must therefore reiterate the message and the signpost: "To increase employment, security, and interna-tionality, schools must incorporate oratory into their curriculum." Is that all? Not at all, it remains the confirmation of the success of the speech.

---

1 Programme for International Student Assessment (PISA) created by the Organisa-tion for Economic Co-operation and Development (OECD). https://www.oecd.org/en/about/programmes/pisa.html

6. Point X - Call To Action (CTA)

Previously, I have explained that the speaker tries to achieve a change in the audience's perception or to encourage a particular behavior. What is distinctive about a *logos* speech is that the speaker must verify on the spot whether they have succeeded or failed.

For this reason, the conclusion consists of two parts. The first part involves asking whether they accept the proposal, for example, with a question or a command: "Raise your hand if you would like me to provide the materials to introduce the subject of public speaking in your school." If the majority raise their hands, the speaker will know they have succeeded. Otherwise, the speaker will need to refine the speech.

7. Closure - *Omega*

The second part of the closure is referred to by Aristotle as *Omega* (the last letter of the Greek alphabet, that is a synonym for the end). It connects the closure with the beginning, to reaffirm the decision that the audience has made.

For instance, if in the initial narrative we have recounted a personal story of failure when speaking in public at a professional meeting, in the closure we might say: "I am convinced that if the schools in our city teach the subject of public speaking, in the future children will not experience the embarrassment I felt at that meeting where, due to my inability to speak in public, I lost such an important project. Thank you very much."

I advise you to use this structure as if it were a template. Have you seen the drawing of the temple above? I recommend printing it out and writing in the spaces to get accustomed to following it step by step.

Later on, you will achieve a fluency that allows you to alter some of the elements, but if you want to speak with confidence and persuade with your evidence, the *logos* is infallible.

An example of a *logos* speech:

* Maty Tchey, a prominent trainer in public speaking, who collaborates in IESE's communication courses, has this video: (https://youtu.be/lcaZwAriE2o) in which she employs the *logos* structure to convince us of the merits of remote working.

* My teaching colleague at IESE, Claudio Hernández, has a straightforward and very visual video (https://youtu.be/KuvWksds9v4), part of a list (https://www.youtube.com/playlist?list=PLdE-Se5mqoK_EoSFIE83WVcZWzu7OBMO6l) of five additional videos by other individuals (in English), which also includes an explanation by Conor Neill, a public speaking lecturer at IESE.

Rafa Martín Aguado

Partner at Rommel & Montgomery, a Spanish consultancy specialising in the education sector, and also at Enigmia, a company that analyses corporate reputation through artificial intelligence. His professional career has focused on corporate communication, particularly in the digital realm.

He teaches communication programs at IESE and in postgraduate courses at the Universidad Villanueva (Madrid).

He holds a degree in Journalism from the Universidad de Navarra (Spain), a master's in Institutional and Political Communication from Universidad Carlos III, and an Executive Media MBA from the Universidad de Navarra.

04.

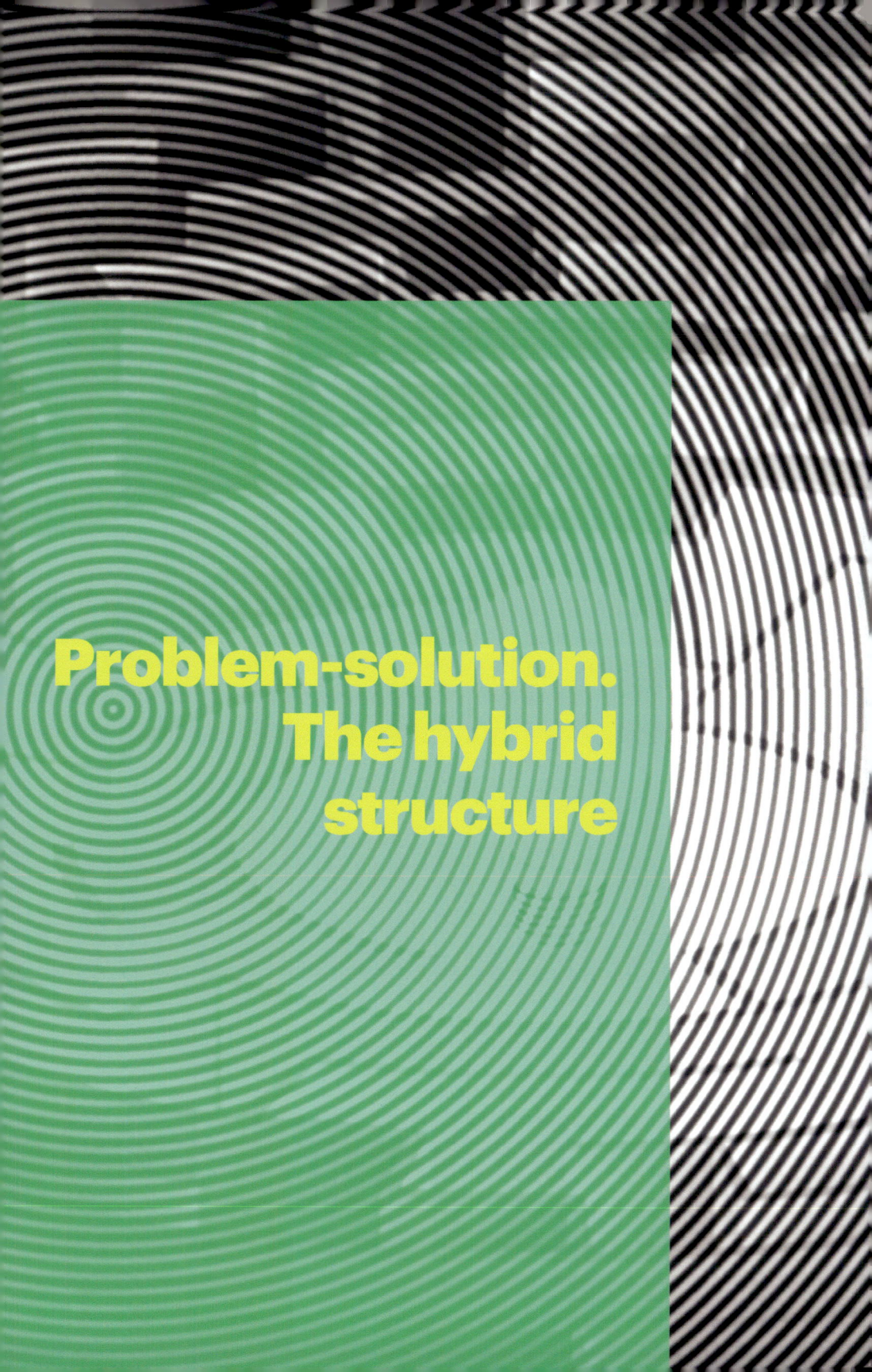

Problem-solution.
The hybrid
structure

"Persuasion is produced by speech when we demonstrate the truth, or what appears to be the truth, based on what is convincing in each case. "

Aristotle. 'Rhetoric', Book I, chapter 2.

Houston, we have a problem! And also, a solution (fortunately)

Within the Aristotelian structures, the Problem-Solution structure dwells just between the *Logos* and the *Ethos*. As a good rational discourse, it is based on data, logic and analysis.

At the same time, it builds credibility: whoever identifies a real problem and proposes an effective solution gains authority in his audience.

In other words, it is not enough to be right *(Logos)*; we must also prove that we know what we are talking about, we understand the context and act with judgement *(Ethos)*.

This mix is powerful because it not only convinces the audience, it gives them reason to trust the speaker.

Why is Problem-Solution *"the Beyoncé* of structures?"

Because it shines, conquers and has stage presence. Among all the ways of organizing a discourse, the Problem-Solution structure is the one that most moves to action. It activates two irresistible springs: discomfort and the promise of relief.

It is the *diva* who does not need to shout to get attention: it shows the pain... and offers the cure. With her, you don't just inform, you transform. So, if you want to convince and generate action, this structure is your best ally with rhythm and charisma.

When someone sits down to listen to you, they rarely think *"how wonderful, I have free time, and I love to listen to other people's problems."* Of course, no. But if you show them that there is something that affects them (or will affect them soon), and that you hold the key to solving it... they stay. And they listen to you.

It's like a good film: it starts with a mess and stays with us until it's resolved. The audience doesn't want theories, they want transformation.

The treasure map: the key parts

The speech with this structure unfolds like a good story: it begins with conflict, follows with tension and ends with resolution. Here are its essential parts:

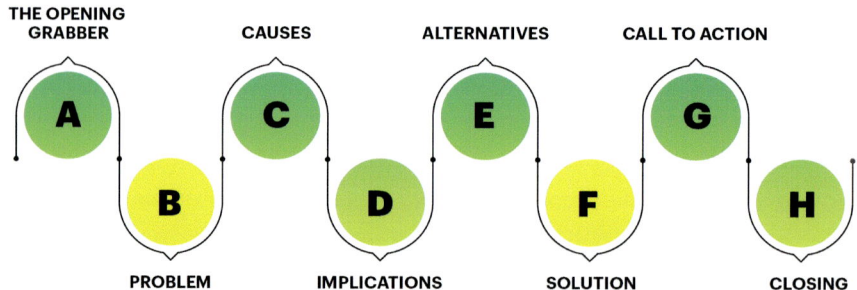

A. The Opening Grabber: to capture attention.

B. Problem: what's going on and why it's important.

C. Causes: where the problem comes from.

D. Implications: what happens if nothing is done.

E. Alternatives: what has been tried.

F. Solution: your big proposal.

G. Call to Action: what they should do now.

H. Closing: what you want them to remember.

A. The opening grabber: capture their attention.... don't let them switch off!

At this point, there are no second chances. If you don't conquer them in the first 20 seconds, the mobile wins.

And how do we compete against the mobile? With an attention-grabbing hook. One of those that makes someone look up from their WhatsApp and think: "Hey, I'm interested in this."

There are many options, but these four, if used well, never fail:

- A surprising fact.

"An adult makes more than 35,000 decisions a day. It's not that we're tired... it's that our brains deserve a permanent holiday."

- A question that shocks.

"Have you ever wondered how much of your life is spent in meetings that could be resolved with a voice message?"

- A personal story with emotion.

"The day I almost lost a client by telling him I was 'already sending him the report' and completely forgetting... I learned that my brain needs alarms even to breathe."

- A phrase with elegant humor.

"Today I want to talk to you about the silent crime in our offices: the air conditioning in Arctic mode while it's 38 degrees outside."

Boom!!! they're paying attention.

B. The problem: where does it hurt?

Once you have got the attention, you can't let it go. It's time to present the problem. But not just any problem: one that hurts, that affects, that matters. Because if they don't feel it, they won't buy it.

The key is to make tangible what it is sometimes presented as abstract.

Don't say: *"There's an internal communication problem."*

Better say, *"In this company, teams learn about changes from hallway rumors... or almost worse, from LinkedIn."*

Some practical advice:

- Be specific. Avoid generalities such as *"in today's society..."*
- Connect to everyday experience.
- Use real, brief examples.
- Provide context without turning it into a lecture.

And an important warning: don't over-dramatize. The intention is to raise awareness, not despair.

Also, forget to look for blame. This is not the time to point fingers, but to raise your eyebrow gracefully.

When you present the problem in a clear, concrete and relevant way, you are opening the door to something very powerful: the need for change.

C. The causes: the root of the problem

We already know that there is a problem. But where did it come from? How did we get here? It's time to do some digging. Without being a dramatic detective, but as someone who understands the roots of the mess.

Your role: to show the causes with clarity, honesty... and without apportioning blame as if it were a meeting of angry neighbors.

Some key points:

- Explain the source of the problem without you turning out like a textbook.
- If you have facts, use them, and do it with purpose.
- If you can tell it with a short story, quite better.

"When the new shift system was implemented, no one explained anything. All that arrived was a confusing Excel and a sentence: 'You'll get organized'. And so began the chaos ...".

This is not the time for pointing fingers. This is the time to understand what happened so as not to repeat it. This is the time to look forward, not to get stuck in "who was to blame."

To show the causes is not to open wounds, it is to prepare the ground for healing. The aim is not to wallow in the past, but to justify logically why we need a new solution.

D. Implications: the future we (don't) want

We have seen the problem and its causes. Now it is time to show what will happen if we do nothing. This is where a powerful tool comes into play: anticipating consequences.

It is not about scaring, but about making it clear that inaction has a price.

The trick is to paint a credible, direct and emotionally uncomfortable future. There is no need to exaggerate. It is enough to be honest and specific.

I will show you some strategies:

- Describe specific scenarios

"Six months from now we'll still be working with the same system... and losing customers to avoidable mistakes."

- Make it visual

"It's like living at the foot of a volcano that has been shaking for years. It seems like nothing is happening... until it does. And then, it's too late."

- Connect emotionally

But be careful: this is not an apocalyptic speech. Don't turn the implications into prophecies of total destruction. The aim is not for people to stand up and shout *"We're doomed!"*, but to think: *"OK, this needs to change now."*

- And as a closing:

"We can ignore it now... but tomorrow the consequences are not going to ignore us."

E. Alternatives: what has been tried... unsuccessfully (or with limitations)

Before presenting your brilliant solution, it is a good idea to show that you know what has already been done, that you have explored other possibilities and, of course, you are not inventing the wheel!

This attitude is important because it builds your credibility. It shows that you don't just jump in with a happy occurrence, but that you understand the situation, you know the other options... and yet you're going for something different.

Some keys to approach this part with elegance:
- Show respect for the other proposals.
- Point out why these proposals haven't worked at all.

'Many tried to solve it by implementing more controls... but that only generated more bureaucracy and less motivation.'

- Use phrases like:

"A common option has been..."

"X has been tried, which has advantages, but..."

"This solution worked for a while, until..."

And remember: don't criticize, contrast. It is not about being the savior who says *"everyone was wrong"*, but the one who says: *"I have learned from what has already been tried... and so I propose something better."*

F. Your solution: your shining moment (without looking like the savior of the world)

Now it's your turn. It's time for your proposal. The big idea. The solution that, after all the above mentioned, makes sense, logical... and even attractive.

But be careful: this is not about selling a miraculous solution, nor is it about going into PowerPoint mode with endless lists. The important thing is to explain what you are proposing, how it works and why it is the best option in this context.

Recommendations to make this part really shine:

- Be clear. Avoid unnecessary technicalities or abstract concepts.

"I propose something as simple as setting up a 15-minute meeting on Mondays to avoid 10 emails during the week."

- Connect your solution to all the above-mentioned.

If you have done your job well, this proposal should feel inevitable.

- If you expect objections, anticipate them.

"You may think this has been tried before... but now the difference is in how it is applied and with what commitment."

- And before closing this section, do not forget to make clear what would be lost if you did not apply this solution:

"Without this system, we will lose our speed, our value... and we will be an expendable team."

Showing what is at stake is another way of saying this solution is not optional, it is necessary.

G. Call to action: move to action (without pushing)

A speech without a clear, concrete and very simple action is like a letter to the Three Wise Men: full of good wishes, but with no guarantee of delivery. Or like a conga of unicorns: pretty but leading nowhere.

You've got their attention, you've shown them the problem, you've broken it down, you've proposed a convincing solution... and now comes the essential part: telling them what to do.

Here is where you need a concrete, realistic and motivating call to action.

Tips on how to build it:

- Be specific. Avoid sentences like "think about it."
- Put a date on it. The more immediate, the better. "We start this Friday."
- Make it achievable. "In 15 minutes, we can set it in motion."
- Focus on this as an experiment "Let's try it for a week and see what changes."

The call to action doesn't have to be grandiose, but it does need to be clear. Don't leave the door half open. Open it completely and point the way.

Example: *"For the next five days, apply this routine with your team. Afterwards, compare the before and after. I assure you that you will notice it."*

This is your gentle push moment. You don't shout "Let's go now!", but you do make it clear that the logical thing to do now is to act.

H. Closing: leave a footprint (not a summary)

You have led your audience on a well-planned route. You started with force, you raised a real problem, clarify its causes, offered a convincing solution and invited them to act.

Now, it is time to close.

Bear in mind, closing does not mean repeating all the above as if we were in a high school essay. It's time to leave an emotional or intellectual footprint. An idea that sticks with them like the last chord of a song.

Ways to close strongly:

- Leave an open question.

 "What if, for once, we all did something different... and it worked?"

- Use a powerful image.

"You don't need to put out volcanoes, you just need to know how to read the signs before they start roaring."

- Or a phrase with flow.

"Convincing is not imposing. It is to illuminate a path that others want to follow."

Close with intention. Not like someone who says goodbye in a hurry, but like someone who gently turns off the light, knowing that he has left something burning in the minds of others.

To conclude...

When we communicate, it's not just about convincing, it's about transforming. The Problem-Solution structure helps us do this. Learning how to use it masterfully is to increase our credibility as leaders by one degree.

Let's go for it!

An example: "The aimless Monday trap"

Grabber:

How many of you have started the week putting out fires... without even knowing what fire you were trying to put out?

Problem:

Every Monday, our teams arrive without a clear idea of what the week's priorities are. That leads to confusion, duplicated tasks... and unnecessary stress.

Causes:

We don't have an agile system for aligning our weekly objectives. We trust that everyone will *"know what's on'*, but that's not always the case.

Implications:

And if we continue like this, we will lose focus, quality and motivation. Each week will become more reactive and less strategic.

Alternatives (already tested):

We tried sending out target emails. But nobody reads them. We made a shared Excel. Nobody consulted it and it ended up out of date.

Solution:

Let's have a 15-minute meeting every Monday at 9:30. Maximum three key points per team. Not one more. Just priorities and the corresponding responsible people. We will review them the following Monday to see the progress and set new objectives for the new week.

Call to action:

We start this coming Monday. I have already blocked the slot in the diary and booked a meeting room – no excuses!!! In 3 weeks, on the last Monday of the month, we will measure if there has been impact.

Closure:

Sometimes changing Mondays... changes the whole week.

Interesting related links:

1. Anne Morriss: "5 steps to fix any workplace problem" (TED Talk). https://www.ted.com/talks/anne_morriss_5_steps_to_fix_any_problem_at_work?language=es

2. Ingrid Kuster: "How to solve a conflict with mediation techniques" (TED Talk) https://www.ted.com/talks/ingrid_kuster_como_solucionar_un_conflicto_con_tecnicas_de_mediacion

3. Andrew Ng: "AI isn't the problem - it's the solution" (TED Talk) https://www.ted.com/talks/andrew_ng_ai_isn_t_the_problem_it_s_the_solution

Pilar Bringas

International speaker and professor at UCM and IESE.

Expert in ethical persuasion and behavioral science applied to business, with a solid track record in corporate leadership, sales and strategy, inspiring professionals and teams to influence with purpose, lead with ethics and convince with science.

05.

Ethos.
The discourse
of credibility

Leadership without integrity is like trusting a false map: can take you anywhere, but not where you should be.

Warren Bennis.
(On Becoming a Leader, 1989)

Marriott President and CEO Arne Sorenson addressing the hotel chain's internal audiences at the height of the Covid 19 crisis.

Ethos. The discourse of credibility

On March 20th, 2020, Arne Sorenson, President and CEO of the Marriott International hotel group, was about to record on video the most difficult communication of his life.

While his team was fine-tuning the technical details of the recording, especially the framing (they were debating how close the shot should be to Arne's face), he was thinking about how he was going to manage the enormous emotion he was feeling at that moment.

Everything was ready. And everyone was ready for the shot, maybe everyone but him, but the moment he started talking the sense of duty flowed from the inside out. The two cameras set up to capture the two angles began to record:

"Hello, Marriott associates. I am here to provide an update on the impact of the Coronavirus or Covid-19 on our business and to discuss the steps we are taking in response to this crisis.

Due to the profound impact Covid-19 is having on so many of us around the world, this is the most difficult message we have had to prepare. Our team was a little worried about making a video now, because of my baldness: Let me tell you that my new look is exactly what was expected as a result of my medical treatments. I feel great and my team and I am 100% focused on overcoming the crisis we are facing."[1]

This speech opening was critical to establishing his credibility. Arne surprised Marriott associates with his image, bald and with a somewhat yellowish skin color. Few knew that he was undergoing chemotherapy treatment for pancreatic cancer. In fact, he died 11 months after this speech, which was intended to explain transparently how the hotel chain was dealing with the measures related to the coronavirus pandemic.

His communication team had debated whether to refer to the illness he was suffering from, although it was really hard to hide the fact that something was wrong with Arne. By confessing, he achieved two hits: the first, sincerity; and the second, transmitted with the example that, despite his physical condition, he was in charge of the business under such challenging circumstances.

This start of speech will be remembered as one of the best examples of crisis communication. It contains some key elements to build credibility: openness, clear and accurate information, sincerity and values. Marriott's chief executive reinforced his leadership just when it was most needed.

The ingredients of trust

In English, the word "trust" has a double connotation: credibility and confidence. Understood as an emotion, confidence is the belief or security in someone or something, which implies the expectation of credibility that will behave positively or that you can rely on it to achieve something. It is created by combining four ingredients: competence, sincerity, credibility and closeness.

In the art of rhetoric, competence is talking about what you know,

---

1 Message sent by Arne Sorenson, Marriott President and CEO to the hotel chain's employees, shareholders and associates on March 28, 2020. https://www.youtube.com/watch?v=LgAMdCV9fxc

that is, technical knowledge of the subject. It is a fairly objective ingredient, as it is easy for an expert in a subject to find out whether the speaker has mastered the topic.

If competence is "thinking what you say", sincerity is "saying what you think." This component of trust is slightly intuitive, as it is not easy to guess what a person really thinks, especially in these times of general disrepute.

Credibility depends on a person's background. It is generated over time. If a person keeps his promises, he has credibility. If he does not keep his promises, he lacks credibility. Credibility is built and, like reputation, it is essential to preserve it. It emanates from the past, from what we have done and how we have done it.

Finally, closeness is a fundamental ingredient in a communicative environment, which nowadays is contaminated by posturing. This term, which means *"artificial and imposed attitude that is adopted for convenience or presumption"* was admitted by the Royal Spanish Academy (RAE) at the end of 2017, at the same time as "post-truth."

This is proof of its abundant use, especially in the sphere of social networks. In contrast to artifice, closeness and warmth connect with the authenticity of the person, a value on the rise in the face of the superficiality that characterizes the communicative environment.

The generation of trust and, therefore, credibility is the objective of the discourse that in Aristotelian rhetoric is known as *"ethos."* Along with *logos* (appeal to reason) and *pathos* (appeal to emotions), *ethos* is one of the three modes of persuasion proposed by Aristotle.

Ethos concerns the moral and intellectual credibility of the speaker, i.e. the image he projects from his thought and work in front of the audience. As Aristotle points out in Rhetoric, *"we should believe in good men more than in others"*.[2] This perspective denotes that the effectiveness of the message depends, to a large extent, on the ethical and professional perception of the sender. In the business context, this dimension is particularly important, as reputation and trust are assets that have a direct impact on legitimacy and influence.

Ethos is not a static attribute, but a discursive construct that must be carefully elaborated. In the corporate environment, it is achieved by demonstrating technical competence, moral integrity and empathetic connection with interlocutors.

---

2 Aristotle. *Rethoric*. Alianza Editorial

A business leader who communicates clearly uses relevant data and acknowledges the concerns of his team not only transmits information but builds a trusted presence. Through tone, language and consistency between message and behavior, an image that facilitates effective persuasion is strengthened.

In addition to its manifestation in the discourse, the *ethos* is strongly influenced by the speaker's trajectory. Organizational and personal reputation, together with a history of ethical decisions, positively influence the public's willingness to trust a proposal.

The structure: past, present, future

Yet, even without an established reputation, it is possible to develop *ethos* in real time through well-structured arguments, the inclusion of credible references or testimonials, and a communicative style that implies openness and respect.

This constant building of *ethos* is especially relevant in multicultural or highly uncertain contexts, where legitimacy becomes a key success factor.

The speaker has to bring from his past experience and learning. What he has achieved is as important as how he has achieved it. It is in the "how" that behaviors rest, which is the best way to validate a person´s value. Consequently, the simplest way to structure an 'ethos' type speech is to begin with the past, apply the learnings from that time to a present situation or challenge and project a good and positive future.

Here is an example of a credibility or leadership speech that follows the proposed structure:

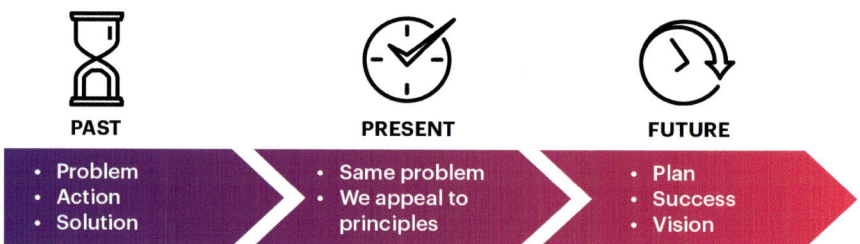

"Colleagues, you have been thinking for a while why I have called you to this meeting without clearly formulating the reason or objective. Am I right? What is going through your minds? A crisis? A salary increment? Neither of those.

I have called you here to tell you that the executive committee has asked us to reduce personnel costs by 20% in the budget for the upcoming financial year. I can already see the expressions of frustration, concern and reluctance.

I would like to remind you that four years ago we gathered in this very room to address the crisis caused by the confinement that led to the Covid 19 pandemic.

I remember those same faces, where concern was prevalent. We had to temporarily close all our shops, put 80% of the staff on ERTE[3], reinforce the online sales team and set up systems to maintain communication with the staff, with our people, in such a difficult circumstance.

And we succeeded it. How did we manage to do it? First of all, by recognizing that the most important thing was people's health and that our first obligation was to take care of them. Secondly, by determining what was essential and leaving out everything else. Thirdly, by strengthening our internal communication systems.

We have struggled to digest the losses caused by that crisis. Today, however, we are a more efficient, more resilient and more focused organization.

If we apply the same principles to the challenge we face now as we did then, I am sure we will achieve the goal. How will we do it? By taking care of people. Let's reduce costs, not people. Let us do an in-depth review of all the budget lines and let us review how we do some things.

I'm sure we do some things that don't add much value just out of inertia.

And let's involve our teams by explaining transparently what we have to do, how we are going to do it and what is expected of us. If we are able to reduce today, tomorrow we will have the credibility to expand our budget. Let's get on with it."

---

3 Temporary Employment Regulation File

The leader offers a vision of the future

On the morning of 3ʳᵈ April 1968, Martin Luther King arrived at the airport of his hometown of Atlanta to board a flight to Memphis, Tennessee, where he was going to give a speech in defense of black civil rights.

King had been in Memphis the previous week to support a strike by black rubbish workers in the city. They were demanding improvements in their working conditions. Among other things, they could not access the showers, because they were reserved for white drivers, nor did they have a place to shelter on rainy days. Now he was back to reaffirm his activist message.

As he settled into the seat, he watched how the aircraft crew moved from side to side. Suddenly, policemen with sniffer dogs burst in. There was a bomb threat targeting him. All passengers were ordered to evacuate the plane quickly. In the end, there was no bomb. The flight arrived an hour late at its destination. It was not the first time he had been threatened, but King remained concerned.

That night in the Mason Temple he spelled out one of his most vibrant speeches. At the climax, he said in an exalted voice:

"Like anyone else I would like to live a long life, but that does not concern me now, I only want to do God's will, and he has allowed me to go up to the top of the mountain, I have looked down and I have seen the promised land.

I may not get there with you, but I want you to know tonight that we, as a people, will get to the promised land. So tonight, I stand here happy, I am not worried about anything, I fear no man. My eyes have seen the coming of the glory of the Lord."[4]

The next morning, 4ᵗʰ April, as he addressed his followers from the balcony of the Lorraine Motel, Martin Luther King was assassinated by bullets fired by a common criminal, James Earl Ray.

---

4 Last speech by Martin Luther King (3ʳᵈ April ,1968). https://www.youtube.com/watch?v=zgVrlx68v-0

In his last sermon he left a magnificent example of a speech of credibility, a message of the future to his followers *"We, as a people, will get to the promised land."*

A leader always offers you the vision of a future worth fighting for. In fact, the purpose of a speech in ethos format is to follow the person.

This is where their power lies: the credibility of the person will be transferred to their arguments and make them more efficient. In fact, former footballer Jorge Valdano argues that *"whoever wins credibility saves words."*

The film *"The Pursuit of Happyness"* offers one of the most emotive endings in the history of cinema. The main character, Chris Gardner, played by Will Smith, celebrates getting a job after a search fraught with frustrations and stumbles.

71

His success began in the first interview he had at the firm, to which he presented sweaty and stained with paint. His sincerity was decisive in generating credibility among his interlocutors.[5]

The audience likes happy endings. In an ethos discourse the future is that happy ending in which converge the efforts of a past whose benefit does not lie in what has happened, but in what we have learned and in the behaviors that we have exhibited that validates the moral values that guide us.

---

5 Scene from the film *"In Pursuit of Happyness"* (2006).
https://youtu.be/UUDKEbX5OQw?si=tRjdxtzooz634Oz7

José Manuel Velasco

The first Spaniard to hold the presidency of the Global Alliance for Public Relations and Communication Management, the world federation of associations of communicators and academic entities, of whose executive committee he continues to be a member as Immediate Past Chair.

Previously he was president of the Association of Communication Managers (Dircom) and the Forum for Ethical Management (Forética). Journalist by training and with a great experience in communication, currently dedicated to the training of managers in communication and leadership.

06.

Pathos.
The emotional speech

"Emotion is the spark that ignites attention, and without attention there is no learning."

Elsa Punset

The *Pathos* Discourse: Speaking from Emotions

"A manager of an automobile spare parts company received a call at midnight: the factory was on fire. Upon arrival, he saw several fire trucks trying to put out the fire. In the morning, when they put out the fire, the factory was almost destroyed.

This manager brought his teams and workers together and gave them an emotional speech to lift their spirits: he told them of all the hardships they had gone through in the past to become a great company. He told them that if they worked together, they could recover in eight months. The speech was so impactful that they recovered in four months."

A well-delivered speech can mobilize people more than anything else in the world. We have seen it in politicians, soldierly, entrepreneurs, managers, organizations...

To create that bridge between the speaker and the audience you have to be able to touch the emotional fibers. There is a name for that: *Pathos*. The term comes from the Greek and means "emotion", "passion", "suffering". Aristotle included it as one of the three fundamental pillars of persuasive discourse, along with the *Logos* (reason) and the *Ethos* (moral credibility of the speaker).

But what is really a *pathos* speech? How is it built? Why do some speeches succeed in lifting the skin, pulling a tear or lighting a spontaneous applause?

This chapter not only explains what an emotional speech is, but also offers concrete tools, real-life examples and practical exercises for any speaker, whether political, academic, business or family-know how to activate that human dimension that turns words into shared experience.

Pathos is the direct path to the heart. It is the connection that goes beyond content, beyond argument, beyond form. It's content with soul. And if used well, it can transform not just a speech, but an entire audience.

A guide to *Pathos*

1. What is *Pathos* and why it works

Pathos does not seek to convince, seeks to move. Appeals to the emotions, sensitivity, empathy of the listener. If the *logos* answers the question "is it logical?", the *pathos* responds to "does it move me?" And in most human decisions, especially the difficult ones, it is not logic that weighs the most, but the meaning we associate with emotions.

Numerous neuroscience studies have confirmed that emotions are essential to decision-making.

A speech that manages to activate emotions gets attention, memory and mobilization. *Pathos* is therefore not only an aesthetic strategy, but a strategic communication tool.

2. When we should use the emotional speech

Although any speech can and should have an emotional component, there are times when *pathos* is the core of the message.

Some ideal contexts for emotional discourses:

- Toasts.
- Funerals.
- Inaugurations.
- Crisis.
- Farewell parties.
- Farewell dinners.
- Celebrations.
- Military parades.
- Award ceremonies.
- Baptisms.
- Weddings.
- Patriotic response.
- Masses.
- Club meetings.
- In memory of meetings.
- Tributes to persons or institutions.
- Victory and Concession speeches.

These motivational speeches are well suited to sports, the business world or teaching. They are also very helpful at times of crisis or collective reconstruction. And they are widely used at the beginning or end of significant cycles in universities and organizations.

In most cases, the aim is not so much to inform but rather to accompany, unite, motivate or give a new meaning to a collective. *Pathos* becomes the way to sustain the collective soul.

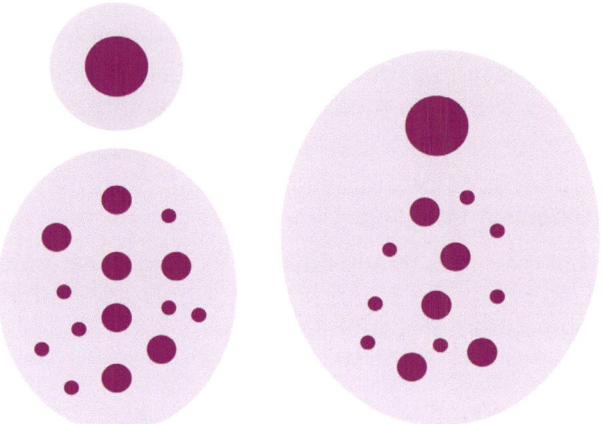

Relation of the speaker to the audience: on the left we have the speech *logos*, in which the speaker tries to argue something to an audience that he has to convince. On the right, in the *pathos* speech, the speaker and the audience form a whole.

3. A proposed structure for *pathos* discourse

Below, you can find a basic structure proposal that can help you generate impact:

A. Context / Reason for the meeting. Situates the moment and its emotional relevance. Make the human tone of the message clear from the beginning.

B. Personal feelings. Share an experience that shows closeness, vulnerability or commitment. Establish a connection from the most intimate.

C. Audience feelings. Recognize what the audience feels or has experienced. Make them feel that you understand what they are going through.

D. Meaning and values. What this moment represents, what values it passes through, what principles are at stake.

E. Path to follow: Propose a realistic but mobilizing call to action that transforms emotion into shared purpose.

Let us consider a hypothetical example from Supermarkets Alba:

We are here because we are united by something more than just a job. We share a story, a purpose that goes beyond the numbers: to provide quality food, with care and responsibility. Today, like so many other times, we find ourselves at an important moment. A change in the organization. And as is natural, we also face certain fears. (Context/Reason for the meeting).

It would not be the first time. When the large retail chains arrived, I thought we would disappear. When we implemented the barcode system in the 1980s, it was a huge leap. I didn't think we would be able to adapt. It seemed to me that it was too complex and difficult. (Personal feelings).

And, what about you? Do you remember the criticism our cashiers faced? Everyone laughed at them, until they began to see that they were faster than competition. What about those who worked in warehouses? They thought they were going to be out of a job because it was changing the way we had been comfortable with storage for decades. And we also changed it. When the customer asked for more fresh products, greater traceability, and enhanced sustainability, you were able to respond. You did it together. Because you were not stopped by fear: you were moved by commitment. (Feelings of the audience).

Today, we talk about technology. Automation, digitalization, new models of work. And also, about uncertainty. But also, opportunity. Opportunity to grow, be more efficient, take better care of our teams and offer more value to those who choose us every day. The difference between resisting and progressing lies in how we remember who we are. (Meaning and values).

At Alba Supermarkets, we are a company that has managed to adapt without losing its essence. And we will do so again. Because what brought us here was not the fear of change, but the desire to do things right. What lies ahead is not the end of our story; it is the next chapter. (Path to follow).

4. Resources of *Pathos*

Pathos discourse is built with several rhetorical and stylistic elements:

- Sensory images: see, smell, touch.
- Rhythm and pauses: allowing time to feel.
- Repetitions: creating intensity.
- Silences: letting the emotion breathe.
- Personal anecdotes: humanizing the message.
- Metaphors and symbols: condensing meanings.
- Rhetorical questions: engaging the audience.
- Sincere language: emotional authenticity.

5. Vulnerability acts as an invisible bond

Showing vulnerability[1] is not a symptom of weakness; on the contrary, it can strengthen the connection with the audience. Chris Anderson, the promoter of the famous TED talks, points out that by admitting insecurities or sharing difficult moments, speakers humanize their message, allowing the audience to identify and engage emotionally.

In fact, one of the most-watched talks in the world is Brené Brown's on vulnerability. She often says that we have always believed that leading was to be strong, invulnerable, always confident. But what most inspires people is not perfection, but humanity. Leaders who dare to say, "I don't know", who ask for help, who listen with their hearts and not just their heads, are the ones who build cultures of trust, innovation, and belonging. "Our capacity to be brave leaders will never be greater than our capacity for vulnerability" (from the book, *Dare to Lead*[2]). Vulnerability, far from weakening the leader, makes him more authentic, more accessible, and ultimately more capable of transforming, according to Brown. It persuades because it excites.

1 https://www.ted.com/talks/brene_brown_the_power_of_vulnerability
2 Brown, Brené (2018). Dare to Lead: Brave Work. Tough Conversations. Whole Hearts. New York. Random House. Page: 12 (English version, hardcover).

6. Real examples of *Pathos* speeches

Example 1: Barack Obama's Speech, 2008

In his presidential victory speech, Obama did not begin with policies or figures. It began with a story: the one of Ann Nixon Cooper, a 106-year-old black woman who had voted that day. With her he covered the 20th century, from institutional racism to the presidency of an African American. It was a secular homily. Hundreds of thousands repeated: "Yes we can." That litany was what turned his victory speech into something very similar to a mass, in which the parishioners repeat the words of the priest. A mass, its homilies and its canticles contain many elements of *pathos*, especially during special celebrations[3].

Example 2: Juan Roig's speech after a disaster

The president and founder of Mercadona, in his first press conference after the catastrophic flood of 2024 (which took many lives in Valencia), stated before dozens of journalists, "A million Spaniards we feel abandoned. The first four days were disastrous. The most affected areas looked like a desert. The only ones who appeared were some companies that stepped up and many volunteers... I get emotional remembering my four deceased businessman friends... The images of the volunteers inspired us... It was the youth who truly engaged, with whatever organization was possible.[4]" His words resonated throughout the country in the news, as they captured the sensitivity and emotions of one of the best businessmen of Spain.

Example 3: General Maximo Decimo Meridio in the movie Gladiator

The General who stars the film Gladiator addresses his cavalry troops before charging at the Germans. *"Brothers. In three weeks, I will be harvesting my crops. Imagine where you want to be, and it will come true. Stand firm, do not separate from me. If you see yourselves riding alone through green meadows, the face bathed by the sun, do not be afraid. You will be in the Eliseo, and you will have died! Brothers! What we do in life has its echo in eternity.[5]"* Many football coaches use this

3 https://youtu.be/_MKXD2pZUhw?si=f0nK6PmqFHhV-1X9
4 https://youtu.be/UaoDH8mrqKc?si=BpTaEPoZHnEIeHV
5 https://youtu.be/CDpTc32sV1Y?si=0F3vhF9nl_sITmPu

excerpt from the film to cheer their teams in the locker room at the most difficult times.

Example 4: Pau Gasol speech in his NBA farewell

The Spanish player who has come the furthest in the NBA, he retired in 2021 and in his farewell speech said: "As a child in Spain, I had a dream. I wanted to become a basketball player and play in the NBA, but I never imagined, not in a million years, that such a day could come. It's a huge honor to be among these great individuals in this great franchise. So, this shows you don't have to set limits on what you can do, what you can achieve, know the best version of yourself every day, as we all know it's the Mamba mentality[6]."

Example 5: Speech by Antonio Banderas on receiving the Goya for Best Actor for Dolor y gloria (2020)

"I am very happy because today, January 25th, it is 3 years exactly since I suffered a heart attack and you have given me this gift to celebrate that new birthday and not only I am alive but I do feel alive[7]. Thank you very much."

7. How to train *Pathos*

It's not about acting. Authentic *pathos* is not rehearsed as a theatrical script but is cultivated from the connection with oneself and the other. To train this type of speech:

- Write about a person who marked your life.
- Choose an intense visual memory.
- Tell the scene in detail.
- Draw a lesson or symbol.
- Read your text to someone close and watch his reaction.

---

6 https://youtu.be/c5LJuv_oHYw?si=olSwGvCvucqmbi4a
7 https://youtu.be/XlgIpNnl2Ck?si=z0OEPVBPluXLdRXF

You can also record yourself. If your voice changes, your eyes become moist or if you need a break, there is probably *pathos*. That is the energy you need to channel when speaking in public.

8. Dangers of misused *Pathos*

Emotional speech can become manipulation if it is forced, exaggerated or made to cry without meaning. A false *pathos* is detected. It causes rejection or cynicism. To avoid it:

- Use real experiences, not made-up.
- Don't prolong unnecessarily the drama.
- Don't seek applause, seek connection.
- Make sure emotion serves the message, not the other way around.

9. *Pathos* in different formats

Not all *pathos* discourses are oral. There are more possibilities:
- Emotional letters.
- Short motivational videos.
- Presentations with symbolic images.
- Testimonial podcasts.
- Advertising with emotional charge.

The principle is the same: activating emotions to mobilize meanings.

10. Conclusion: what is left when the words go out

When a speech ends, it remains what was felt more than what was said. *Pathos* is the emotional memory of the message. And therefore, although it is not always the most rational thing, it is usually the most remembered.

Learning to speak with emotion is not learning to cry in public, it is learning to tell truths that matter. It is learning to look into the eyes, to count with the soul and leave a mark that goes beyond the speech.

In short, a well-constructed pathos discourse does not need great effects or grandiose oratory. It just needs truth, emotion and a structure that allows that emotion to be shared. Because in the end, the best speech is one that not only is heard but felt.

Summary

1. Emotional connection with the audience.

The speaker should show "empathy", understand the feelings of the audience and reflect them in his or her message. This creates trust and closeness.

Example: "I know many of you have lost what you most wanted...".

2. Personal narratives or human stories.

The "real or symbolic stories" touch the heart of the listener. A good emotional speech is based on anecdotes that humanize the message.

Example: "I remember a mother who told me in tears that...".

3. Sensory and expressive language.

Words that evoke "images, sounds, smells, emotions" are often used, reinforced with pauses, tone and rhythm. How you say it is as important as what you say.

Example: "The silence in that house was louder than any scream."

4. Appeal to universal values.

Pathos works best when it connects with deep values like "love, justice, loss, hope, family or dignity." This elevates the discourse from the individual to the collective.

Example: "We do not fight only for ourselves, but for those who will come after."

Dr. Carlos Salas

He has been director of El Economista, Capital, Metro and lainformation.com. He was editor-in-chief of the section of Economy and International of El Mundo.

Professor of Communication at IESE, EAE Business School, IMF and La Salle.

Professor of Journalism in the Master of Journalism of El Mundo. Author of "Storytelling, magic writing", and "How to speak and present in public". Degree in Journalism and Philosophy. PhD in Philosophy.

Storytelling.
The art of telling
stories

JAWS

"Storytelling is the most underrated skill in business.

Ben Horowitz

Good business stories should make your audience feel that they are about to be devoured by a wild animal, and then feel a huge relief when they are not. Steven Spielberg, who is a master at the art of storytelling on the poster of his first blockbuster reflects exactly that moment.

ROY SCHEIDER **ROBERT SHAW** **RICHARD DREYFUSS**

JAWS

Make everything unforgettable with stories

The venture capitalist Ben Horowitz says he won't invest in a company that cannot explain itself with a simple story, and that the CEO is actually the chief storyteller. He likes to say that your story is your strategy.

A lot of people think this means you make a strategy and then storify it. Actually, it's all one step. Your strategy should always be easy to repeat. Humans are hard-wired to remember and retell stories; they are programmed to forget complicated mission statements, statistics and jargon-filled corporate values.

The companies he has invested in Airbnb, Slack and Instacart, have not just given him outsized returns, they all have a strategy that most consumers understand.

Most effective business stories have a structure closer to fairy tales and jokes than to epic movies.

It's a structure as old as time, from Aristotle to Pixar, and it has three main blocks (SCR):

(S) Situation: Tell the audience the minimum they need to understand the story: when, where, who. Tell them what normal looks like. Pixar designs every story beginning with "Once upon a time..." "Every day..."

C) Complication: Stories are boring without conflict. Pixar's prompts for this stage are "But one day..." and "Because of that..." and "And from then on..." There was a normal before and a new normal after. Our hero faces a challenge that gets harder and harder.

(R) Resolution: Pixar's prompt for this is "Until finally..." Even if the hero doesn't solve the problem, the audience has a lesson to take away from the story.

Storytelling Structure

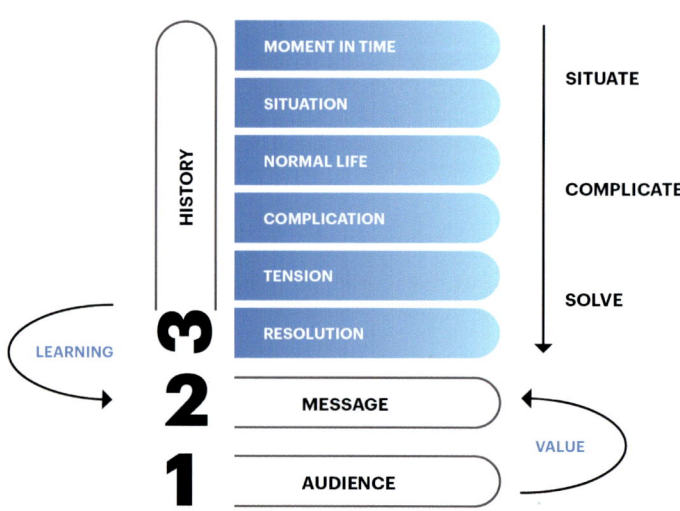

The learnings and the takeaways are what make the story valuable. And by starting with the message most valuable to your story, you determine which story is best to tell.

The problem for most leaders is that they assume that their offices and business plans are too boring to be turned into stories. In this chapter we'll see how the opposite is true. Business leaders like Warren Buffett and Steve Jobs can make anything interesting – an email, a pitch deck, a reply to a question on a panel – by turning it into a story.

Start a Story When the Bear Is About to Eat You

Let's start at the beginning. The physicist Carl Sagan once said that to make an apple pie, your first step is to create a universe.

That's way too early for any story, but that's how the beginning of a lot of business presentations can feel. You get nine slides of background information and methodology that feel pointless, followed by a conclusion.

Think of the situation as the minimum the audience needs to know to understand the story, and then think of the complication that transform it. Most TV shows start with the complication, then return to the opening situation. The marketer and personal branding expert Wes Kao recommends when writing memos on any topic to your boss that you should imagine it's a story and that you should "Start any story where you are just about to be eaten by a bear." In a business context, this could be a representative customer about to leave your company, an opportunity about to be missed, a painful bug that seems small but is undermining your company. Whatever will fill your audience with suspense will work to make them pay attention to the resolution and your message.

Start With the Lesson And Find a Hero

There is another element to every good story: people. You need a person in the center of the story and need the audience to relate to the person.

Warren Buffett spends most of his time analyzing statistics and company reports, yet expresses with stories more than numbers. In a typical Berkshire Hathaway report, only about 10% of the total word count is dedicated to numbers, the other 90% is dedicated to telling stories, with a clear principle attached to each story.

Throughout his career, Buffett has always found a way to attach a person to a number. For instance, rather than give a flat return on investment figure in his 1977 report, he creates a small portrait of the founder of the company:

"Gene Abegg formed the bank in 1931 with $250,000. In its first full year, earnings amounted to $8,782. Late last year Gene, now 80 and still running a banking operation without peer, asked that a successor be brought in." Situation: Guy buys a bank. Complication: It is tiny and regional. Resolution: It is incredibly profitable and still regional. Message: You should invest in long-term consistent returns anywhere they happen.

Buffett storytelling

WORD COUNT OF HIS 1977 LETTER TO INVESTORS
CUMULATIVE NUMBER OF WORDS

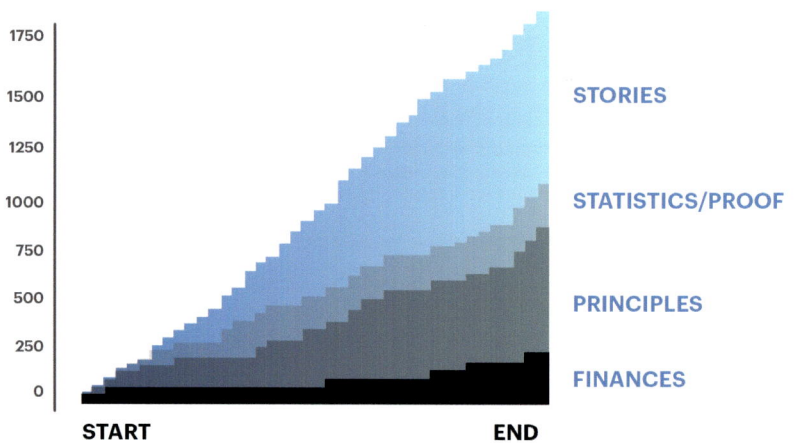

Add Emotional Contrast

Most business people assume that success is what grabs attention. But constant success is boring. Stories need a complication.
The writer Kurt Vonnegut had a simple way to diagram stories. Vonnegut shows that as storytelling has become more sophisticated, the plots involve large and frequent swings from high to low. This is your

complication and your way to build tension, as a general rule aim for a happy ending. Fear gets attention, but optimism promotes action.

Emotional contrast in stories

KURT VONNEGUT ANALYSIS

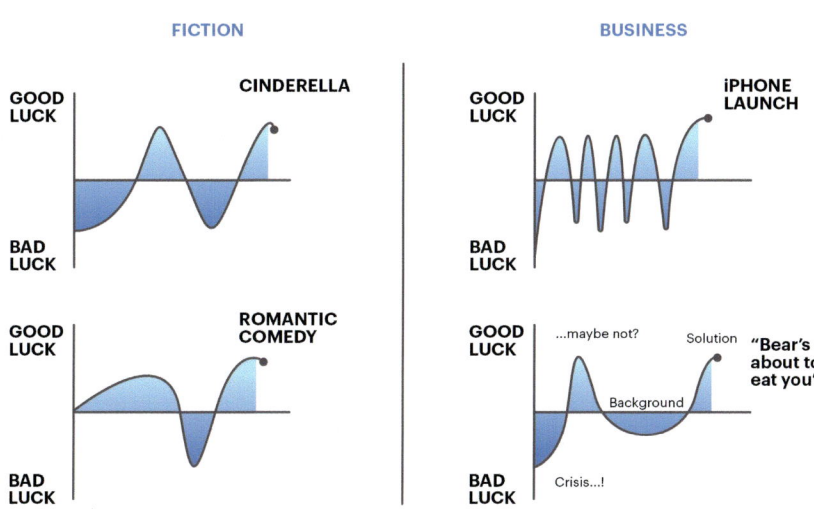

Shorten Your Stories to the Essentials the South Park Way, or Launch an iPhone

As a rule, the ideal length of any story is... shorter. Most people will try to reduce a story by cutting words, but what you should focus on are beats.

If you love telling a story or joke, you already know that as long as you cover a few key moments, the story is complete. If you expand your story, you don't add new moments, you add in details about particular moments to add tension during the complication...

Paying attention to how these beats connect will show you how to sharpen your story.

"We found out this really simple rule," said Trey Parker. They write out the beats of the story. Then they see what words connect them. "If the words AND THEN belong between them, you got something pretty boring."

Instead, they ensure their beats are connected by one of only two words: BUT or THEREFORE. The BUT comes when an event complicates things or makes it difficult. A THEREFORE is when the next part naturally follows.

This approach also allows you to vary the emotional tone, as Vonnegut demands. The speech writer Nancy Duarte analyzed hundreds of effective speeches from politicians and business people that inspired change.

The speaker would discuss the problems of the present, then switch to a vision of an amazing future, and then return to the problematic present, and then to an amazing future.

Whether it was Martin Luther King Jr. or Steve Jobs, the speech ends with one simple solution that brings the future away. Alternating between BUT and THEREFORE has both this emotional impact and creates a sense of momentum in your story.

Putting it all together

Now that we have the concepts of beats, emotional range, a principle, connections, and a good place to start, let's see how Jobs and Buffett used them in two very different contexts.

The first is a selection of beats from Steve Jobs launching an iPhone and the other is Warren Buffett being asked for life advice by young people.

The first was tightly scripted, and the second was improvised. In both cases, however, the structure of their stories is the same.

	Steve Jobs iPhone Launch – Beats Connected	Warren Buffet – Q&A on life lessons
OPENING-COMPLICATION About to be eaten by a bear	Every once in a while, a revolutionary product comes along that changes everything. Before we get into it, let me talk about a category of problems.	You're going to face setbacks, (Buffet investing partner) Charlie and I faced setbacks. And I can't tell you they're fun.
SITUATION - NORMAL LIFE The lesson and the reason to tell the story	Smartphones are a little smarter than regular phones, but they actually are harder to use. They're really complicated.	You're going to have good luck and bad luck. And people who have good luck tend to think it's themselves when it's luck...
AND THERE-FORE	We solved this problem. So how are we going to take this to a mobile device? What we're going to do is get rid of all these buttons and just make a giant screen.	If you're born in China today, you're amazingly lucky compared to 100 years ago. Or a thousand years ago. Your only real choice in life is to be a rice farmer, which I could not do.
BUT	How do we communicate with it? We don't want to carry around a mouse, right? So what are we going to do? Oh, a stylus, right? We're going to use a stylus. No. ... Yuck. Nobody wants a stylus. So let's not use a stylus.	Bad things do happen. It hasn't really happened with me, but with my friends it has. The biggest setback we all face is death, of course. And it's no laughing matter. I can't offer advice about how to have "the time of your life" when setbacks occur.

AND THERE-FORE	We're going to use the best pointing device in the world. We're going to use a pointing device that we're all born with – born with ten of them. We're going to use our fingers. We're going to touch this with our fingers. And we have invented a new technology called multi-touch, which is phenomenal.	You still can focus on good luck. Athletes today make so much more money than they did 20 years ago. I love to watch them. It's a new style of playing now. Sports gets better.
BUT	We want to reinvent the phone. Now, what's the killer app? The killer app is making calls! It's amazing — it's amazing how hard it is to make calls on most phones.	Even that can feel really unlucky if you didn't make the cut for a basketball team. And Charlie and I are not athletic. We're totally unfit. We eat terribly.
AND THERE-FORE	Let's say I want to make a call to Jony Ive. I can just push here, and I see Jony Ive's context, with all his information: his three phone numbers, his e-mail, whatever else, his address, whatever else I've got. It's all in one place. And if I want to call Jony, all I do is push his phone number.	We're both lucky to be alive today where, despite never exercising, we can outearn athletes in this day and age and live long lives. So despite our health setbacks, and other setbacks, we're lucky to be alive today.

CONCLU-SION- RESO-LUTION	The lesson and the reason to tell the story, again. So we're bringing breakthrough software to a mobile device for the first time. It's five years ahead of anything on any other phone.	Remember the good luck, no matter what you face in life: you're incredibly lucky to be born now and not a hundred years ago.

Picking Stories and Practicing Storytelling

We know that literally, a child can do this. So why do so few entrepreneurs do this?

Storytelling is more of a muscle than a set of rules. This muscle atrophies in a business setting and especially at the start of a career. But there is another training that will give you financial returns like storytelling. Here's a training plan:

- Commit to tell a story at least once a day. There are opportunities to tell a story in every email you write. Think about the message, then a story of change that shows it.
- Look for stories constantly, and share them as soon as you can. Look for those Vonnegut extremes: any time you are stressed, furious, excited, relieved, nervous, pumped, amazed, there is usually a story. Tell someone else about this moment as soon as you can, or record it as a voice note.

- If you're on deadline and need to find a story fast, then it's best to start with the principles you live by and then tell the story of how you believe them.

Ask yourself:

- What do I know that no one else knows?
- Where was I when I first realized this?
- Which were the events and experiences that made this seem so important to me?
- Who else do I know who has benefitted from this knowledge?
- Who else do I know who has suffered because of the lack of it?

- What's the scariest situation my audience could be in if they don't listen to me?
- What's the most exciting situation my audience could be in if they do?

In an age where everyone can get AI to write well from them, your stories are one of the few things unique about you. Your stories are the most effective way to break through that noise, to connect with an audience, to make your ideas meaningful and memorable, to share emotion, and to lead. AI might be a better storyteller than you in terms of technique, but it has no stories to tell. You do.

Videos

- Kurt Vonnegut: The Shape of Stories:
(https://www.youtube.com/watch?v=GOGru_4z1Vc&t=336s)
- Nancy Duarte: Common Structure of Greatest Storytellers:
(https://www.youtube.com/watch?v=1nYFpuc2Umk)
- Steve Jobs: Love, Loss, Death: Commencement Address at Stanford:
(https://www.youtube.com/watch?v=UF8uR6Z6KLc)

Robin Moroney

Robin uses stories to cut through the noise of social media and the fog of AI-created content.

A former editor at The Wall Street Journal, he uses a mix of coaching and data science to give leaders the confidence that everything they say will have an impact. He was a speech writer for Google CEO Sundar Pichai and ran Google's Asia comms strategy.

He is currently based in Madrid and, alongside his consulting practice, publishers a newsletter about writing with AI tools called "The Message is the Medium" in partnership with the AI consultancy "Road to Amherst."

08.

The voice.
Paraverbal
communication

" The human voice is the most versatile musical instrument ever created.

Ingo R. Titze

"

When the Scottish Susan Boyle first appeared, in April 2009, in the TV Britain's Got Talent Contest, it was not her appearance or the chosen song what lifted the audience from their seats. What moved audience was the use he made of her powerful voice.

Master your voice and connect with others: A practical guide

Introduction

The voice is like your footprint: unique, unrepeatable and very powerful. When we speak, we don't just say words. We also show how we feel, how confident we are, whether or not we believe what we say.

The voice can calm, excite, bore or inspire. It is your best ally to communicate better... but sometimes we don't train her or give her the attention it deserves.

In this guide, you'll discover how to use your voice more consciously and effectively. You just need to practice a little each day.

1. Mind-body connection: knowing yourself from the inside

Speaking is not just using your mouth. Everything that happens inside you is noticeable when you speak: if you are tense, your voice shrinks. If you are relaxed, your voice flows. That's why **knowing your body from the inside is so important**. It's not just about moving or stretching, it's about paying attention to what you feel, what you think and how you express it.

Mind-body connection involves being present, realizing how you react when faced with a situation that requires public speaking, and using that information to improve. If you are not in tune with your body, you can feel blocked without knowing why: you lack air, your mouth dries, your heart accelerates... and all of that directly impacts how your voice sounds.

The goal here is not to eliminate all emotions, but to learn to **listen to the body and work with it.** When you have body awareness, you can better regulate your nerves, breathe more deeply, maintain an open posture and project your voice more confidently. It's the first step to using voice as a powerful communication tool.

Practical tips	Why does it serve?
Stretch out as if you were waking up	Activate your body and release tension.
Walk a few steps breathing deeply.	Calm the nervous system
Take 3 deep breaths through your nose.	Focus your mind and body before you speak.
Roll your shoulders back 10 times.	Improve posture to better project your voice.

2. Breathing well is speaking well

Breathing is the basis of a **healthy, clear and powerful voice**. Without it, it is very difficult to hold long sentences, project without shouting or maintain a fluid rhythm. Most people breathe superficially, using only the upper chest. This causes fatigue, neck tension and a voice that sounds weak or choked.

Conscious breathing is about **paying attention to how the air comes in and out** and training yourself so that the breath flows from the abdomen (the area of the diaphragm). It is sometimes called "breathing with the belly", and although at first it may seem odd, it is the most efficient and natural way of breathing to talk.

Also, **breathing well helps you to be present**. It reduces anxiety, gives you a sense of control and focuses you before you speak. If you breathe fast and choked, your brain interprets it as a warning situation. Instead, if you breathe slowly and deeply, your body understands that everything is fine... and so does your voice.

Mastering conscious breathing is not only useful for the voice: it makes you feel calmer, firmer and with more scenic presence.

Exercise -The invisible whistle:

Inhale for 4 seconds and exhale as if you were whistling, but without making a sound, for 6-8 seconds. Feel the air coming out in a controlled way. This trains your exhalation, key to speaking well.

Practical Tips	What is it for?
Place a light book over your abdomen as you breathe.	You will feel if you are using the diaphragm correctly.
Imagine you are inflating a balloon from your stomach.	It will help you visualize the correct expansion.
Exhale as if you fogged a mirror.	Activate your hot and controlled air.
Count from 10 to 0 while slowly exhaling.	Train the duration of your spoken phrases.

3. Prepare your voice as if you were a singer (even if you are not)

Have you ever tried to speak in public without warming up your voice? It's like going out for a run without warming up your muscles: you may survive... but you can also end up with a broken voice, without air or talking like a robot.

Your voice also needs to warm up

You don't have to be a singer. Just spend 2 or 3 minutes to activate it: move your jaw, make soft sounds, yawn loudly or hum your favorite song.

Think of it this way:

In the same way that you stretch your body before exercising, **warming up your voice prepares your instrument to function with ease and energy**. And if you don't... you risk to lose your voice just when you need it most.

That´s why it's a good idea to do some quick exercises before any presentation or class.

Phrases with intention:

Say phrases like "I'm here and I have something important to say" marking each word with energy. Do it slow, then fast, then with different emotions.

Practical Tips	What does it improve?
Make your lips vibrate: "brrrrr."	Releases tension in the face and jaw.
Hum a song in low voice.	Activates your resonators gently.
Open your mouth wide when you say "la-la-la-la."	Improves articulation and volume.
Yawn several times.	Relaxes the throat and activates the natural voice.

4. Speak clearly to be understood

It is not enough to have a good idea or a great message. If the way we say it is not clear, the message is lost.

The **articulation** is simply to move the mouth, lips, tongue and jaw well so that the sounds come out defined.

Diction is saying the words correctly, without swallowing syllables or speaking too fast.

When we do not articulate well or pronounce in a hurry, people may have to make an effort to understand us. And if they have to do it, they will probably disconnect.

This point becomes even more important if you are in a large room, giving class or talking on video call (where audio quality can play against you).

A good articulation makes your voice sound more professional, safe and clear, no matter where you are. It also improves your confidence. Because when you know they understand you, you feel more comfortable talking.

Pencil trick:

Place a horizontal pencil between your teeth and read text out loud. Then repeat without the pencil. Do you notice the difference? It's a quick way to improve clarity.

Practical Tips	**What do you get?**
Read texts aloud every morning.	Improves fluency, articulation and confidence.
Talk in front of a mirror for 5 minutes daily.	Observes your gestures and movements when speaking.
Use tongue twisters like " *She sells seashells by the seashore.*"	Improves oral agility and concentration.

5. Give rhythm and music to your voice

Have you ever heard someone speak without changing the tone, without pauses, without emotion? Do you remember how hard it was to stay alert? Exactly: monotony is the worst enemy of an interesting voice.

The rhythm, pauses, tone and intonation make your voice come alive. That's what is called **musicality**. You don't need to have a radio speaker voice or be an actress; just **vary a little how you speak** to maintain attention and convey emotions.

When you use rhythm and musicality well:

- Avoid sounding flat or robotic.

- Keep the audience's attention.

- Energize important ideas with pauses and tone changes.

A good pace does not mean talking fast or slow. It means knowing **when to accelerate, when to brake and when to be silent**. Silence also communicates. Sometimes a well-placed pause says more than a hundred words.

Reading with a metronome:

Use a metronome app and try to read in sync with the rhythm. It will help you keep a steady cadence and improve your control.

Practical Tips	What is it for?
Read a story as if it were a play.	You practice emotions, pauses and changes of rhythm.
Highlight with colors when to pause or emphasize.	You guide your voice like a movie script.
Record yourself reading and listen whether it sounds flat or expressive.	You detect monotonous patterns to correct them.
Play to tell a story with different emotions.	You exercise your expressive and persuasive capacity.

6. Project your voice without breaking

Speaking loudly is not shouting. **Projecting the voice** is making people hear you clearly without sounding forced or aggressive. And this is achieved by **good breathing, posture and resonance**, not by squeezing the throat.

Many times, we try to speak louder only with the voice, and that ends in tiredness, aphonia or discomfort. On the other hand, when you project well:

• Your voice reaches farther without effort.
• You sound more confident and authoritative.
• You can talk longer without fatigue.

A good projection comes out of the body, you need to have the correct posture, with open chest and using air efficiently. You don't need more strength; you need **better technique**.

In addition, a projected voice generates presence. Whether you are in a room with 30 people or in front of a camera, if you project, you **make yourself noticed**.

Resonance exercise "mmm": Make a "mmm" sound as if you were tasting something rich. Feel your face vibrate. That vibration means your voice is resonating well. Practice it every morning.

Practical Tips	What do you get?
Imagine you're talking to someone in the back of the room.	Improve direction and strength without shouting.
Read a paragraph by increasing the volume of each sentence.	You train the volume control.
Maintain a firm posture: feet apart and open chest.	It helps the air flow, and the voice expand.

7. Put emotion to what you say

Your voice not only informs. It also excites. And when you are able to **transmit emotions with your voice**, you connect much more with those who listen.

We often say important phrases, but with a flat tone, and therefore they have no impact. Other times, we repeat a learned text, but without putting an intention... and it does not generate anything. What differentiates an authentic voice from a mechanic is the **emotion behind it.**

The emotional expression has to be consistent with what you're saying. If you talk about something sad, you can't sound happy. If you're telling something inspiring, your tone should go with it. That's noticeable. You feel it.

Working on your emotional expression is **connecting with what you're saying before you say it**. You must feel it first so that others can also feel it.

And overacting is not necessary. Sometimes it is enough to do a small change in tone, a pause or a word said with the intention of touching emotionally the listener.

Listen to others:

Watch TED talks[1], speaker videos, movies. See how they use voice to transmit, imitate them, then find your style.

Practical Tips	Why does it matter?
Tell a personal story with real emotion.	Connect to your most authentic natural tone.

1 https://www.ted.com/

Practical Tips	Why does it matter?
Use pauses before saying key phrases.	Generate emotional impact.
Imagine talking to someone you appreciate.	Change the intention with which you use your voice.
Practice reading a sentence as if it were a movie scene.	Train emotional expression and drama.

8. Nerves: the elephant in the room

Feeling nervous before speaking in public is totally normal. It's not a defect; it's part of the process. The important thing is to learn how **to manage these nerves so that they do not block** you but play on your behalf.

The body reacts: sweat, trembling, shaking voice, mind blank. But if you understand that this is just **unchanneled energy**, you can make them play on your behalf.

The key is to prepare your body and mind for what's coming. Breathe well, move before you speak, visualize that you're going to be okay. It's not about eliminating nerves (that's almost impossible) but about **turning them into action**.

And the more you practice, the less power those nerves have. Because your body will start to feel familiarity, and experience will replace fear.

Breathing 4x4:

Inhale 4 seconds - hold 4 - exhale 4 - pause 4. Repeat 4 times before going out to talk. Your body is regulated, and your mind is calm.

Positive visualization:

Close your eyes and imagine that you are speaking with confidence, that the audience is listening to you and connecting. Practice this before going to bed or before talking.

Real mini rehearsal:

Practice with someone you trust or record yourself on video. Even if you're embarrassed, it's the best way to improve and gain confidence.

Practical Tips	What do you get?
Repeat as a *mantra*: "I'm ready, my voice is clear".	Strengthen your mind before you begin.

9. Final summary and action plan

- Breathe with your diaphragm every day.
- Do 5 minutes of vocal warm-up before you speak.
- Take care of your pronunciation by reading aloud.
- Play with rhythm, tone and pauses.
- Connect with what you say and who you listen to.
- Turn nerves into impulse.

The voice as a communicative tool

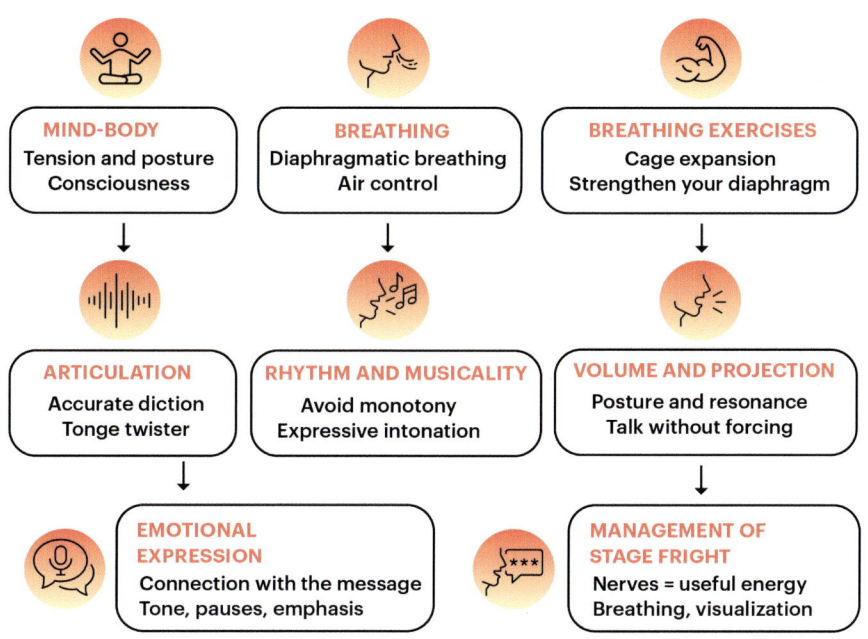

And above all: **enjoy it**. Because when you use your voice well, they don't just hear you. They feel you.

Videos:

- Diaphragmatic breathing exercise (https://youtu.be/0Ua9bOsZ-TYg)
- Breathing to control anxiety (https://youtu.be/p8fjYPC-k2k)
- How to express emotions with voice (https://youtu.be/elho-2SOZahI)
- NEVER Feel Anxiety Again When Giving A Speech (5 EASY Methods) (https://youtu.be/Edg54WnYqkE)

Bibliographic references:

1. Arushi, undefined, Dillon, R., Ni Teoh, A., & Dillon, D. (2022). *Voice analysis for stress detection and application in virtual reality to improve public speaking in real-time: A review*. [PDF]

2. Ayres, J. (1996). *Speech anxiety as a social phobia: Behavioral treatment and strategies. Communication Education*, 45(3), 234-246.

3. Banse, R., & Scherer, K. R. (1996). *Acoustic profiles in vocal emotion expression. Journal of Personality and Social Psychology*, 70(3), 614-636.

4. Becker, D. R. (2019). *Vocal manifestations of reported past trauma* [PDF]

Dr. Ana Fernández Jiménez

Career Coach | Speaker | Former Director of HR International.

With more than 20 years of experience in Human Resources and talent management, she has helped thousands of professionals to develop their personal brand and enhance their corporate impact at Hazzlo.es.

As a teacher and consultant, she combines practical strategies with innovative leadership and persuasion. She has worked with companies such as BBVA, Louis Vuitton and Airbus, providing solutions in strategy, training and organizational development. Its practical and realistic approach inspires professionals to stand out and communicate with impact in a competitive world. Speaker TED Talk.

Non-verbal. Public speaking tips

" Non-verbal language is the first to reach us. "

Mónica Pérez de las Heras

Eight non-verbal communication tips for speaking in public

I am sure that when you have had to prepare a speech in front of your team, the board of directors of your company or in a meeting with clients, you have spent hours and hours preparing what you are going to say: the main messages, the data or the actions you expect from your audience. But you have hardly spent time preparing your non-verbal language: i.e. gestures, expressions, attitude, where to look, and so on.

Well, after reading this chapter, that cannot happen again. Record the following in your mind: **it is not only important what you say, but how you say it.**

There is no doubt that what we say with our words has an obvious relevance in our discourse. But just as significant, if not more so, is the way we communicate it through our body language, attitude and tone of voice, among many other things.

Don't worry. Public speaking is a skill that can be developed with training and, above all, with a lot of practice. And with these 8 tips you will make your speech much more impactful, effective and authentic.

1. Move around the stage to emphasize your message

One of the most common questions when speaking in public is: do I have to move, or can I stand still? Without a doubt, movement can energize your message, make it more enjoyable and help you highlight certain aspects and ideas.

Don't be afraid to move around and use the available space on a stage. In general, moving around is good, but it's not about moving around just because you have to. It must be coherent with your message, with what you are saying.

For example, imagine you want to confront two ideas or points of view, or a conversation between two characters or between you and another person.

You can present one idea (Idea 1) to the right and the other (Idea 2) to the left of the stage. With minimal displacement, your audience will know which idea you are referring to.

You can also move to set different ideas, arguments or parts of your speech.

You can, for example, say one argument in one place, move on, move forward a bit and stop for the second argument or idea to be given in another place, and so on. Or use this structure to place different time slots in a story.

As in everything, we must avoid excesses. If the space is small, don't move just by or making little circles, because that can make your audience dizzy and even transmit that you're nervous.

Another very useful tool is to approach our audience, because that denotes proximity, and the audience will feel more involved during the speech.

When we want to highlight something or make it clear that something is very important, there are several resources: one is to step forward and launch that idea or argument.

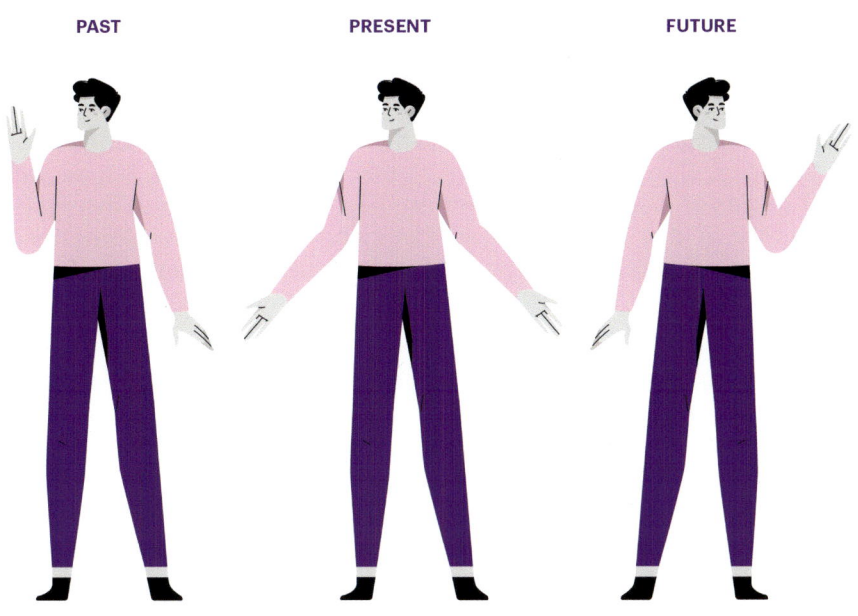

Another, for me the most effective, is to stand and throw it –always with a tone of voice and gestures that emphasize it even more–. Because then your audience will know that the idea is really important.

Don't be afraid to use resources like screens and whiteboards and move towards them to highlight a fact or idea and then return to your audience. And remember something fundamental, you never turn your back on them.

2. Put passion and energy in everything that you say

If you're not excited about what you say, the listener won´t either. Therefore, it is very important that you are passionate about the subject you are going to expose because if it really moves you, you will transfer it to your audience.

When there are inconsistencies between what we say and what our body says, the message that prevails is our body language. So, if we want the people who are listening to us to be on the same emotional level, we must transmit that level of emotion.

You may wonder, how do I do this in front of the steering committee? Or my boss? Sometimes we have to talk about technical issues, difficult topics or issues that are not entirely aligned with our interests. Always try to look for something that connects you with something that excites you, and that will help you give more impact to your message. Try to emphasize it and you will communicate your emotion.

Preparing your presentation by pointing out what energy you want to give each part of the speech is a trick that helps a lot. But be careful, do not confuse passion and energy with speeding up when you speak, making many gestures, abuse of hand gestures or speaking very loudly. No, it's not about that. In fact, this can ruin your speech because if it sounds too forced, you're not going to be credible and much less shocking.

3. Posture

Remember: **our body language communicates more than our words**. That's why your posture before your audience is crucial, whether you are sitting or standing. With proper posture you will transmit confidence and security. Why? Because you will feel more comfortable and confident, as it allows us to breathe better, be more relaxed and communicate our emotions and energy more effectively.

A good posture is to have our feet firmly on the ground, with our body firm but relaxed, pulling the body up. The chest in front open, which transmits openness to your audience and will allow you to breathe better. Open your arms because it gives confidence and security and a high head, looking straight ahead.

It is not a question of maintaining always this position like something static, but to be aware that you have to feel secure, rooted in the ground, with a firm, open and prepared posture. As we saw in point one, the movement helps to reinforce our message and reach out more to the public, but this is the "basic" stance that we return to after any voluntary movement.

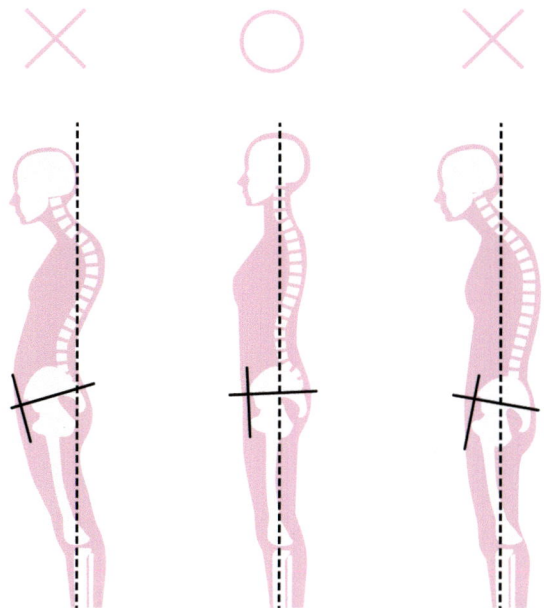

Try to avoid putting weight on a hip, being hunched or low, because you risk of generating in your audience rejection, insecurity or even anger. Look for a posture that conveys confidence, security and openness to your audience.

4. Hands, your great allies

Arms and hands can help us say many things: to emphasize an idea, to stress the main message or to contrast two different aspects.

The hands are great allies to show change in the rhythm of our speech, or tranquility; to communicate closeness or separation, or authority and firmness. For example, a very common gesture is to put them together in the middle with fingers connected to emphasize the main idea.

By opening them, we transmit openness and transparency to our audience (Image 1) and we can use one or the other to emphasize an idea (Image 2), or to list some points of our speech.

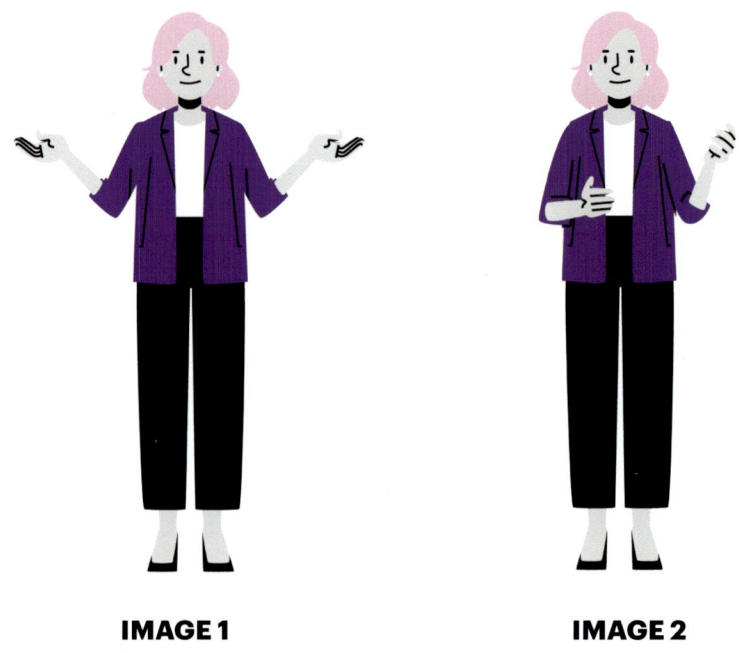

IMAGE 1   **IMAGE 2**

5.   Don't be afraid of pauses and silences

If we want the audience to follow us and understand the concepts and ideas that we transmit, we have to give them time to assimilate. In this sense, pauses and silence -yes, silence - are very useful tools that can help you communicate more and better.

A good technique is to remain silent for a few seconds at certain moments of your presentation or speech, because it helps to highlight that moment. Stop on purpose, with a precise intention gives much strength to our speech: announces that something new is coming, helps us anticipate something important, or an element or crucial fact that our audience can´t miss.

In addition, taking a short pause can help us to breathe deeply as we discussed in the previous section.

And along with controlled pauses, there is silence, which can help us generate interest, give more emotion to what we are doing or even attract the attention of those who are distracted. Launching a certain message, a reflection or question to the audience and then silence is a practice that helps a lot to oxygenate the speech and connect again with our audience.

The silences and pauses also help us to avoid pitfalls like *"mmm"'* or *"and"* or any throat clearing very common when we talk in public. These repetitions arise unconsciously because our mind needs to think about the next idea we want to expose. Stop a few seconds, a brief silence is much better than hearing these filler words because they can become annoying if we abuse them.

Another very useful practice is to leave a long silence at the beginning of our talk. This will help you to generate interest, confidence and credibility. It is also a very useful resource when there are people in the room who keep talking even though you are starting your presentation (either in an auditorium, but it can also be in a meeting or in a class). So, hold on a bit until there is absolute silence and then it starts off with a shocking kick.

6. The power of the gaze

In communication, remember that the most important thing is not you but your audience. It is imperative that you think about them: who they are, what their interests are, how you can best reach them so that you get your message across. And eye contact helps us a lot to connect with them.

Think that where your gaze goes, so does your communication. Sometimes, our insecurity makes us lose consciousness of our gaze and this leads us to direct the view to the floor, to the ceiling or just to the screen where we project our presentation. This makes a lot of difference to your message. An open, kind, sincere look at your entire audience conveys a lot.

Try to consider everyone, that does not mean to look around the entire audience but direct it to specific people to connect.

A good trick to avoid getting nervous is to look for people who smile at you, who are paying attention to you and that they reassure you. There are always some people like this among your audience but never forget the rest.

Turn your gaze to all of your audience

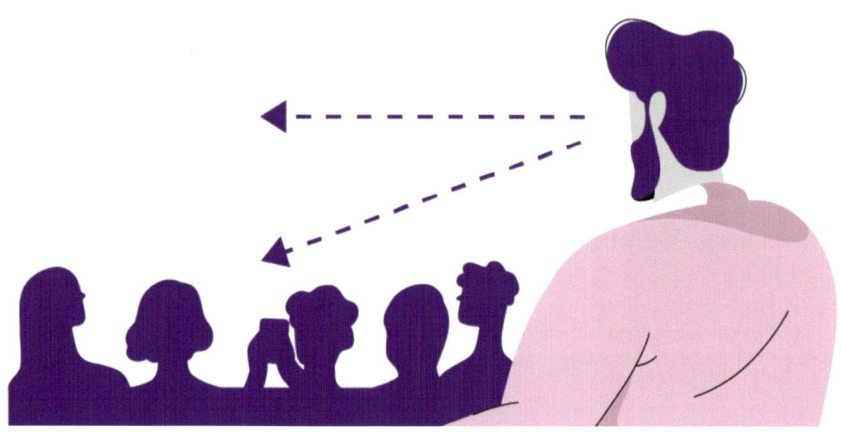

Your gaze when you speak in public is a great tool to integrate all those who listen and connect with them.

7. Smile

The first thing that connects with the audience is our gesture, the expression of our face. People who smile at us attract us more. Therefore, always try to start and end your speech with a smile because your audience will be more likely to pay attention.

But it is not a matter of smiling without meaning, and it should not be a forced smile. It is a tool that brings us closer to the audience by showing us friendly, safe and open.

You do not have to be smiling all the time, in fact, the most advisable is to adapt the gesture of our face to what your exposure requires: smiling if what we are counting is neutral, serious when the issue deserves it or sad if the circumstances require it.

So, start and end your speech with a smile, but along the way stick to what reinforces your message.

8. Don´t read your speech

In public speaking training courses, it is very common for participants to ask their trainer, during their presentations, to have their laptop, mobile phone or paper with their speech or notes on it close at hand.

They are afraid of not being able to develop it well or forget what they mean. They feel insecure and some of them become very nervous if they do not have something on hand to turn to in case they lose the thread.

I always ask them to have nothing, and they realize that, in the end, they can do it without any kind of support.

The key is to prepare the speech, to practice, to repeat it again and again until we master it. Think that no one knows better than you what you want to transmit, that you are the only one who knows what you want to talk about.

With all the tools we teach you in this manual and, above all, with a lot of practice, you will be able to make a great speech, and you will not need any paper.

Looking at your notes now and then is not bad, but you have to be aware that your speech loses strength the more you read. And you may become a boring, robotic speaker. Think of the great speakers, none read.

On the contrary, they continuously maintain eye contact with their audience, to reach them better and avoid a monotonous and boring speech.

Practice, practice and practice

Public speaking is a skill that everyone can learn. Nobody is born knowing everything. Preparation and practice are the keys to be able to acquire that skill. It's like riding a bike: Once you learn, you don't forget.

Whenever you have to speak in public, consider all these tools and practice, practice, and practice. You can do this in several ways: "using" your partner, children, friends or anyone else to rehearse your speech and get feedback. Or recording you with a camera (the mobile one is good) so that you can see and analyze all the aspects we have seen.

Take any opportunity to speak in public. Don't be afraid of it, the more you do, the more you will grow: a business meeting, an intervention to your team or your clients, even a family meeting where you can give a short speech.

And most importantly, think that YOU can.

Go for it!

Beatriz Toribio

Graduated in Journalism, Beatriz Toribio has extensive experience in press, radio and television. She was part of the founding team of *El Economista* and has presented and directed her own TV program specialized in the real estate sector.

Thanks to this outreach work, it has been awarded several awards and is Top LinkedIn Voices since 2021. Her professional career also includes corporate communication in Spain and abroad, as well as the training of speakers for professionals from different sectors. Since 2021 she has collaborated with IESE in different programs for managers and communication courses.

10.

Crisis.
The crisis
discourse

> **The best of leaders is not the one who does great things, but the one who leads his team to do great things.**

Ronald Reagan, US president (1981-1989).

Crises are the moment of truth, the time when we can see what we are made of. In crises we discover heroes like Chesley 'Sully' Sullemberg (on the right), the pilot who in 2009 managed to splash down in the Hudson River with his damaged plane, saving all his passengers and crew. We also recognize villains like Francesco Schettino (on the left), the captain of the Costa Concordia cruise ship that capsized in 2012 due to his recklessness, and who was responsible for the death of 32 people.

The crisis speech

If in normal situations a good leadership is expressed by speaking in the first person about the needs of a society or an environment, about the company's plans and objectives, and about one's own and others' motivations and resistance, in a crisis situation, the need to face up to and explain what is happening is even more pressing.

In these circumstances, it is essential to communicate convincingly with your own team, other employees, shareholders, customers, public authorities, the media and those who follow you on social networks. Everyone needs to see that we are aware that there is a serious problem and that we are doing everything necessary to solve it. In crises, silence does not work.

However, crises bring a great deal of tension for those who have to speak in public: expectations are disproportionate, fears of misunderstanding multiply and internal and external pressures are enormous. People expect us to tell them immediately clearly what is happening, even though those in charge rarely have all the information... It's hard to have the nerves of steel not to be carried away by emotions, especially when the company's activities have caused casualties.

To make matters worse, each crisis is like a fingerprint: no two are alike. Is it possible to have a blueprint of what you should say in a critical situation?

The answer is affirmative: we can propose an outline of a crisis discourse because, although the specific business response varies according to the circumstances, what does not change are the questions we have to answer. Our stakeholders always have the same concerns, expectations and apprehensions, which must dictate the content of our discourse and even the order of what we say.

Step 1: Repudiate the damage caused by the crisis

The first element of the response is intended to *connect emotionally with the audience*, eloquently expressing that it repudiates what has happened, which is always bad.

Those who listen to us want to feel that they regret what happened and the damage caused: not whether we are guilty or responsible for the facts, but that they hurt us... Even if we have nothing to do with them.

At this early stage it is also appropriate to connect what is happening with corporate identity and purpose. This means that we not only regret that someone suffers but that it affects us, because we defend the value that is injured in that suffering: that it hurts us that a worker has been hurt because he is one of ours, but also because the safety of our employees is fundamental to us.

Depending on each crisis, the principle to which we appeal is different: freedom, defense of customers, integration and the fight against discrimination, care for the environment, etc. This mention is important because it provides a framework of interpretation (it is not something that is wanted or even less frequent, but an accidental exception), not only for outsiders but also for insiders.

Step 2: The narrative

The following step is an *explanation of what happened*, which serves as an official interpretation of the facts. It should provide a logical narrative of what has happened, the causes involved and what is being done at present.

During a crisis, there are different versions of the facts, which compete with each other. That´s why it is important for the institutional version to succeed, for audiences to make it their own and repeat it, because the narrative conditions the interpretative framework and the role of the other actors in the public scene.

A narrative is not just a chronology of events, but goes beyond: it assigns roles to the protagonists. In a story there are heroes, villains, victims, witnesses, authorities, experts... The roles are fundamental; they define what our role is in what happens.

People do not process data but emotions. Sometimes they seem to ask: what has happened here? But deep down what they are thinking is: which side am I on? That's why it is so important to provide the data with the narrative.

In this narrative, we tell what happened in chronological order, distinguishing what we know for sure, what is probable, and what we do not yet know and are going to investigate.

We should not be embarrassed to admit ignorance: on the contrary, we should reject the temptation to present ourselves as if we were in control of the situation.

Step 3: Operational decisions

The speaker then lists the specific actions that the organization has taken, or is considering taking, to deal with the crisis. They are at the same time actions and communication: they are taken and communicated, because that is the only way to be effective. And he only mentions the objectives: each case will require different initiatives.

a) *Actions to resolve*

The first are aimed at *solving the problem* immediately: take immediate measures to stop the negative effects on victims and on the public, and block the domino effect: stop the production of a product under investigation and announce the collection of those that were sold; entrust someone with the care of the victims (e.g. arrange for their relatives to travel to the site of the incident); remove from their duties the persons allegedly involved, etc.; and do so without delay.

The material part is important, but the emotional does not lag behind... and sometimes we forget, or we think it's private and that organizations should not get into, and they don't. In the face of the acute pain of the loss of loved ones, it is relevant to facilitate mourning, which is partly private and partly public.

This is well known in public institutions (state funerals), but less so in companies. Therefore, respecting the privacy, religious freedom and wishes of people, we must know how to offer them, so that they decide what, how and when.

b) *Measures to investigate*

The second initiatives are aimed to *find out what has happened and its causes*. When the facts and what caused them are not clear, it must be decided and announced (in this order) that an investigation will be undertaken to clarify what happened, and that the organization is determined to get to the bottom of the matter (if it is involved, of course...).

Where the authorities take the lead in responding to the crisis (a train accident, for example), the investigation is also carried out by that authority. In these cases, the organization decides and announces (in this order) its full cooperation with the official investigation. Only internal investigations for aspects not directly related to the accident are possible.

For example, the railway safety authority will investigate whether the damaged locomotive had passed all the revisions and the spare parts were approved, while the owner company should investigate who and why original spare parts were not purchased.

The same is true for fraud: the police will investigate whether the company manager had accomplices when he stole money from the cashier, but the organization will review the process of selection, recruitment and training of that manager in case there are there has been negligence, or simply to punish and improve.

When the facts are private, then responsibility for the investigation lies with the organization itself, unless the stakeholders are able to suspect that the organization's leadership is involved by action or omission and therefore could remove evidence that commits them. In this case, the investigation should be entrusted to independent third parties. Otherwise, it will be difficult for the results of the investigation to be credible.

c) *Reform measures*

The third set of decisions addresses *internal reform*: what needs to be changed in the organization so that it cannot happen again.

Some frequent measures in this field are changes in the processes of selection of people, stricter protocols in the contracting of goods and services, increased safety measures for employees, improvements in quality controls, etc.

d) *Measures to restore justice*

The fourth group of measures to be announced concerns *damage to natural or legal persons* or to the community as a whole.

In some cases, it will be tried to return to the previous situation, when this is possible (for example, if a sausage factory contaminated a river, it must clean up and recover it). In case of offenses to someone's good name, one must return the fame to the one who was unjustly offended. And when the lost cannot be recovered, compensation for the harm caused must be offered.

Restoring justice also means that, once responsibilities have been proven, the guilty are punished by action or omission. Punishing the wrong behavior is an inseparable part of justice.

Sometimes the sanction that a company can impose may be only symbolic: for example, withdrawal of an award. But symbolic sanctions are extremely important, because they speak for themselves of one's own priorities.

e) *Corporate renewal measures*.

The last group of measures aims at *renewing the corporate culture*: recovering the fundamental institutional principles and values which gave rise to the institution.

These measures are necessary when the actions that caused the crisis were very serious breaches of public trust. So, it is not only necessary to reform, but to proceed to a kind of refoundation, which provides a new vitality and a renewed sense of mission to the staff and other priority audiences around the original identity of the institution.

Examples of such measures include in-house training programs, the drafting of a code of ethics, changes to the incentive system, etc.

Step 4: Closing

The crisis speech ends by recalling the identity principles that inspire the organization, which were already explained at the beginning. It is like a promise to those who listen to us, because in a crisis it hurts what happened, but it worries above all what will happen in the future. They need to hear from us who we are, because in crises not only those who know us well listen to us, but the dramatic events attract the attention of many others who do not know us.

Finally, we announce how and when we will provide more information: for example, a forthcoming press conference, a dedicated website on the evolution of the problem, etc. The response to crises is not instantaneous, it develops over a period of time, and we have to satisfy the right to know of our stakeholders.

So far, the structure of the crisis discourse. But we should bear in mind that what counts most are not the words of those who speak, but their actions. The effectiveness of crisis discourse is based above all on credibility. The formal perfection of speech matters, but even more so anything that inspires confidence in listeners.

Dr. Paulina Guzik

Combines journalism and academia. Heads the international OSV editorial team. Previously she hosted a weekly program on TVP, the Polish television; worked in the news departments of three TV channels, including CNN in New York. Covered elections from the US to Russia and conflicts, including the Russian intervention in Georgia in 2008.

As a professor, she teaches and researches in communication at the Pontifical University John Paul II in Krakow, Poland.

She has experience in advising companies as a communication consultant, especially in the coal energy sector (*Węglokoks Energia, Kompania Węglowa*), as well as medical institutions (outpatient clinics and hospitals).

She holds a PhD from the University of Warsaw (2015) and a master's degree in journalism (2006) and international relations (2007) from the University of Warsaw.

11.

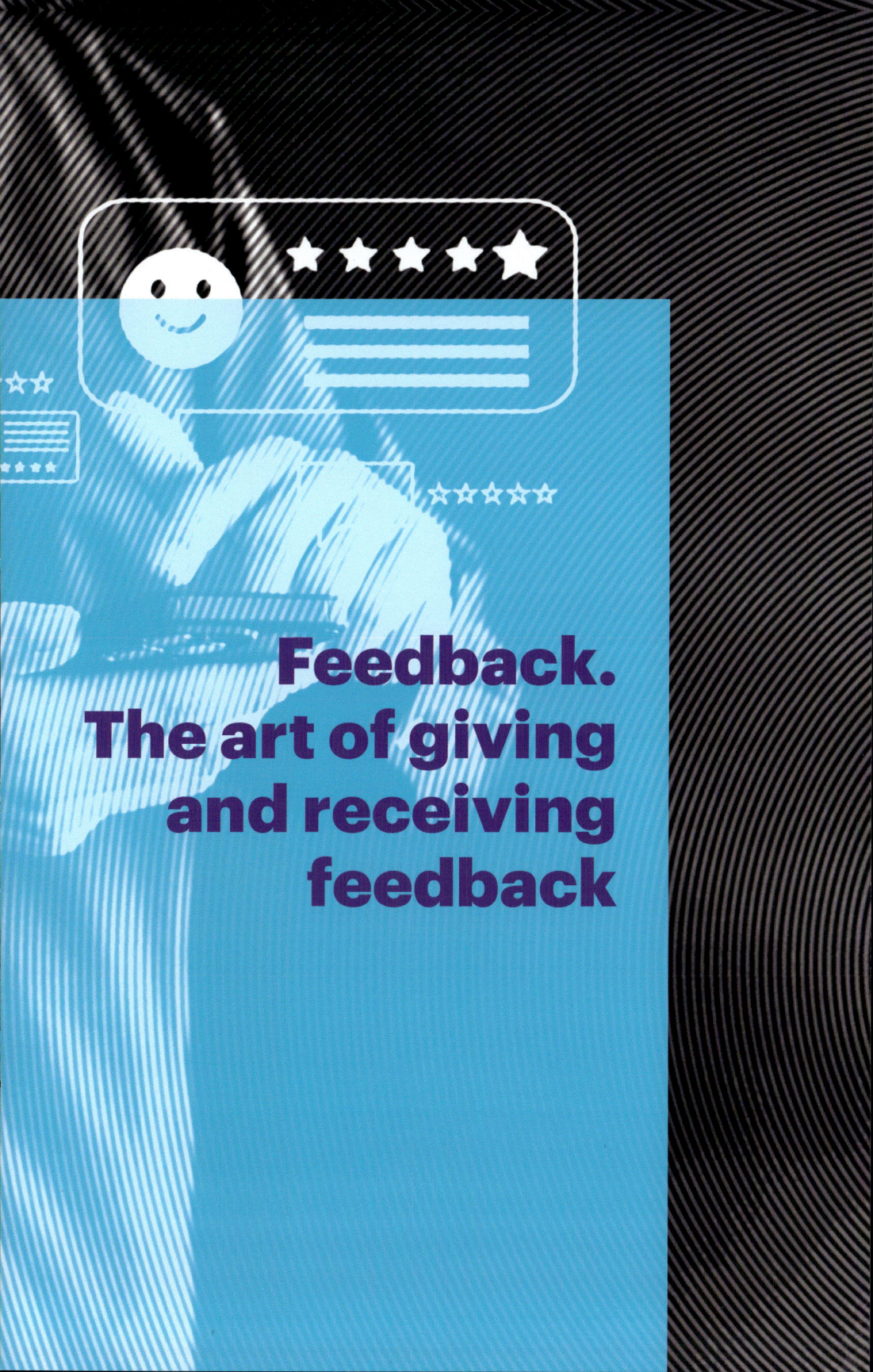

Feedback.
The art of giving and receiving feedback

"What we have to learn to do, we learn by doing.

Ethics to Nichomachus.

Aristotle "

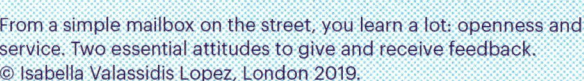

From knowing to doing: the power to give and receive feedback

You are reading a communication manual and have reached the last chapter. The rules of oratory have become clear to you. You know about structure. You know the basic principles of communication. You can distinguish the types of speech. You know what body language implies to communicate.

You know. You know a lot.

But let me tell you something you may not expect; knowing is not enough.

Knowing the rules of oratory, mastering the structure of speech or understanding the technique of body language does not guarantee that we know how to apply it fluently. The gap between knowledge and practical competence is wider than it seems. In fact, it is easy – even without wanting – to fall into an illusion of competition. The

Dunning-Kruger effect, a cognitive bias described by psychologists David Dunning and Justin Kruger in 1999, shows that people with little ability tend to overestimate their abilities[1]. The best remedy is to test what we know in reality.

Practice makes master. But blind practice is a long and slow journey. If we want to move quickly, we need a tool that tells us what to improve next time and teaches us how to detect it for ourselves. That tool is the feedback: all the information we receive about ourselves that helps us see more clearly how we impact others and how we can grow.

The feedback – that return of the boomerang – allows us to look at the most important dimension of all communication: the other as protagonist.

Do you want to learn how to speak in public? Learn how to give and receive feedback: about the oratory of others and also about your own. That's the virtuous circle of feedback: accepting it, processing it and incorporating it freely. And in that gesture, we become more capable of listening, analyzing, and being able to provide useful feedback to others.

1. Receiving feedback

If in communication the protagonist is the other, then in the feedback it is who receives it. Therefore, before learning to give feedback, it is necessary to learn how to receive it.

Being good communicators means being willing to listen, accept and incorporate feedback, starting with the informal one, which comes from the audience as we speak. Are you attentive to their gestures, laughter, silences? In the *Friends series*, episodes were recorded in front of a live audience, and if something didn't work, the writers would screen the scene. As comedians, we must learn to read and react to that live feedback.

Then there is the formal feedback, which we receive at the end of an intervention. It is normal to feel like a threat: We become defensive, look for excuses. But those reactions are only the first reflection.

---

1 Dunning, D., & Kruger, J. (1999). *Unskilled and unaware of it: how difficulties in recognizing one's own incompetence lead to inflated self-assessments.* Journal of Personality and Social Psychology, 77(6), 1121–1134.

The most important thing is what we do next, our second reaction: how we process observations to grow.

In communication, perceptions are more important than facts. Therefore, listening to how others perceive us and acting accordingly is an essential tool for improvement. With time and practice, the gap between the first and second reactions is narrowing. Just as the actors in *Friends* became funnier by understanding their audience, we become better communicators when we incorporate what others perceive of us.

Our disposition

The other day, playing *hide-and-seek* with my two-year-old daughter, I counted to ten and when I opened my eyes, she was still there, curled up with her blindfolded eyes right next to me. "Elena, honey, just because you close your eyes doesn't mean I can't see you."

Sometimes we act like this with ourselves: we avoid facing each other, as if that would save us from being seen by others. But not seeing is not the same as not being seen. That's why, when we talk about feedback, we talk about humility.

The word comes from *humus*, ground. And to be humble is, at least, to have your feet on the ground, to know yourself truly: both the shining and the polishing.

A humble person allows himself to see his whole reality. And that openness makes any process of improvement more direct and effective. On the other hand, living with our eyes closed -blind to ourselves- makes us slower, insecure and reactive. it takes us away from growth.

Tips for getting feedback like a professional

Listen actively: listen inside and out. Without interrupting, turning off the inner monologue that rebates the speaker. Listening to understand, not to answer. Even when we disagree. Listening is moving forward.

Take notes and reflect later: there are ideas that at the moment we cannot understand, but days later *they clicked on you*. Taking note gives us the opportunity to see patterns and discover the path of improvement that we have achieved thanks to the advice of others.

Thank: saying "thank you" is always the best answer. We do not give feedback on received feedback. Developing the habit of appreciation is one of the best ways to encourage people to keep giving us valuable notes.

Implement it as soon as possible

The quicker we put into practice the advice given to us, the better we will be able to understand the recommendations. It is an easy way to compare the difference in results more accurately[2].

Generate opportunities to receive feedback

A good speaker is recognized by his openness to feedback. He seeks it, provokes it and thanks it. He doesn´t wait for it to come, he asks for it. Create your own feedback network. A network of people you can count on to give you valuable feedback.

Sheila Heen, co-author of the book "*Thanks for the Feedback: The Science and Art of Receiving Feedback Well*" recommends avoiding asking feedback with the generic question "do you have any feedback for me?", instead of, she recommends asking specifically, in our case it could be: "*Could you tell me something that you see me as hindering my presentation?*".

The ideal thing is that the questions you ask will change over time according to your goals for improvement.

2. An improvement lever in oratory: observe and analyze

To help you analyze the speech of others, or your own interventions, here is a simple guide.

The Radiography: A practical guide to analyze a speech:

A. Start: A good start not only presents the topic, generates expectations, opens doors.

2 Kolb, D. A. (1984). *Experiential learning: Experience as the source of learning and development*. Englewood Cliffs, NJ. Kolb argues that learning is consolidated by transforming experience into action, and that applying what is learned immediately strengthens understanding and retention of knowledge.

- *Did the speaker catch my attention from the start?*
- *Was there an effective "hook" (a question, image, data or story that made me want to keep listening)?*

B. Body: Here we observe the internal logic of speech, its ability to hold itself in order.
- *Did the speech follow the proper structure?*
- *Was the message consistent throughout?*
- *Did you use clear transitions between sections or ideas?*
- *Was the time spent on each part proportional to its importance?*

C. Closing: The last thing we heard and the first thing we remembered.
- *Was the ending memorable?*
- *Was the whole speech consistent from start to finish?*
- *Did it leave me with a reflection, an image or a call to action?*

D. Form: Form also communicates. Sometimes, more than the content.
- *How did you use your voice? (volume, rhythm, pauses, intonation)*
- *Did the body language (gaze, gestures, posture, command of space...) accompany and reinforce the message or contradict it?*
- *Was the speech of appropriate duration?*
- *If you applied, did you use visual aids or criterial support materials?*

E. Impact: The real proof of a speech is in its footprint.
- *What emotion did the speech cause me and the rest of the audience?*
- *What idea did I get recorded?*
- *What do I remember a few hours later?*

3. Giving feedback: an act of service

Giving feedback is an act of service. It involves humility to recognize that we are not the protagonists, respect for the person in front of us and an active listening that allows us to understand where he is and how we can help him move forward from that point.

The feedback should be...

Concrete and specific: Avoid vague phrases like "the speech was good" or "I wasn't convinced." Provide precise examples that allow the other to identify what worked and why. Remember that the purpose of feedback is to guide the practice to be quality. Saying "I liked your talk" does not help. Saying "you managed to cap attention from the beginning by using a personal anecdote", yes.

Balanced: Highlight successes and point out improvements with clear proposals. It is essential to give space to the strengths to reinforce them and enhance what naturally gives good to those who have in front of us[3].

Timely: The best time to give feedback is when the experience is still alive in memory. The emotions are fresh and the details present. Always keep in mind that there are recommendations which is better to give only privately.

Customized: Feedback is not one size fits all. Some people appreciate direct feedback, and others need a more progressive approach. Good suits are made to measure.

Encouraging: Giving feedback is one way to tell the other things like: *I believe in your ability to grow*. The one who gives good feedback becomes an expert in discovering the potential of others. Giving feedback, even when pointing out mistakes, is always a positive act: it seeks to open paths, reinforce strengths and accompany the growth of the other.

An effective format for giving feedback

Unlike a logos speech, feedback does not have an accurate and infallible structure on which to base itself. There are times when the feedback may be only a recommendation for improvement and reinforcement of a strength because we consider it sufficient for the person we are caring for.

However, there is a very usual and quite simple structure that we can follow: it is the 3x3 technique: three aspects that worked well, three aspects to improve.

---

3 Drucker, P. F. (1999). *Managing oneself. Harvard Business Review*. Drucker underlines that knowing your own strengths and working from them is much more effective to try to compensate for weaknesses. Improving what we already do well may us from good to excellent with much less effort.

An example of such a format would be:

"(+) I liked your ability to connect with the audience from the start, using a moment in time that moved us exactly where you were. (++) You also manage to keep the narrative tension by masterfully using the suspense by not telling us who was responsible for what happened. (+++) Your closing was inspiring, you brought us back to the moment at the beginning, making an omega closing that allowed us to close the circle and be surprised by the resolution of the conflict.

Now, to improve the speech, (-) you could work on slowing down the pace at key moments using some silences, (--) you could better interpret the figures with a more powerful intonation of the voice, to give strength and importance to the numbers, that in the case of your speech can not lose strength next to the story (---) take care of the movement of your hands, remember that movements also speak and if you make gestures without meaning or unconsciously, distract your audience.

Excellent work! You have a talent for telling good stories, you can force what I comment on and see how your ability grows (motivating closure)."

4. More real-life examples

Example 1: Feedback to a nervous but clear speaker

Laura gave a talk about emotional education using the ethos structure or "leader's speech". She was visibly nervous, but her content was deep and her structure clear.

Feedback:

"Laura, you connected with your subject in a very authentic way and gave us specific examples of your professional work. You used the past-present-future structure in an appropriate and linear way.

You should work on using more pauses to breathe and project calm, remember that the faster we speak the more we transfer the feeling of nerves. Another aspect to work on is that you spend more time of the speech in the "future". You spend a lot of time in the "present" describing the problem, that your audience already knows it, and very little outlining the outcome and benefits of implementing your proposal.

Your message is coherent, and if you manage to accompany it with a presence to accompany him with a serene presence, he will gain strength. You are your message, courage!".

Example 2: Feedback to an enthusiastic but messy speaker

José presented a business idea. His energy was contagious, but the speech was disorganized in several moments.

Feedback:

"José, you have a drag energy, look at the audience, you approach the audience, you master the space.

I encourage you to spend more time planning the structure of your speech, the story that should go from point A to point B, you give too many twists, and we have lost in the way. Summarize and synthesize the story to better reflect your business potential.

The energy and confidence you have need a single speech structure logos to reflect the reasons why your product is better than others. If you also use the tools of storytelling for the opening it will be the perfect combination so that your strength and your enthusiasm have a clear channel and not dilute your message."

5.   Practical exercises

Individual exercise: *Dialogue with your own voice.*

Objective: Strengthen self-perception and train the capacity for self-assessment based on objective criteria. **Duration**: 15 minutes.

Instructions:

1. Record a short speech on a subject you master that lasts between 3 and 5 minutes.

2. Look at it twice: The first, without taking notes. Just observe, applying active listening on three levels: emotional, technical and strategic. The second applies the previous evaluation guide (start, body, closure, shape, impact).

3. Write:

• Three things you did well (with specific examples).

• Two concrete areas for improvement.

• One action that you will implement in your next intervention.

Optional: Repeat the exercise a few days later with a new recording and compare.

Group exercise: *The impact thermometer*

Objective: To train critical listening, formulation of specific feedback and receptivity to group feedback. **Duration**: 45 minutes.

Instructions:

1. A volunteer presents a topic for 3-4 minutes.

2. The rest gives feedback to the speaker.

3. Everyone has a turn to present and receive feedback from the group.

4. Once everyone has spoken, each one says which comment was most useful.

5. Each person writes an action that he commits to implement in his next intervention.

Conclusion:

"What we have to learn to do, we learn by doing," said Aristotle.

I hope this chapter has been an invitation to you to turn knowledge into action, and action into habit. Knowing is not enough: we need to practice, observe, listen, correct and try again.

Feedback, in all its forms, is the *omega*, the closing of the circle, the information we need to bring our "doing" ever closer to the goal of becoming excellent communicators.

Film (or short video): **The King's Speech**.

A spectacular film and a great example of how the feedback, applied with sensitivity and constancy, can unlock the communicative potential of a person. The whole movie is valuable, but an alternative is to watch this short clip (https://youtu.be/7WJtsOgKCRM)

Clip (duration 4 min. approx.): **Mr. Keating and Todd's poem**.

A heartwarming scene in which Professor Keating (Robin Williams) guides a student to find his own voice. His feedback is a brilliant example of how to create a safe, encouraging and challenging environment at the same time (https://youtu.be/IrvMrf-Pjhw).

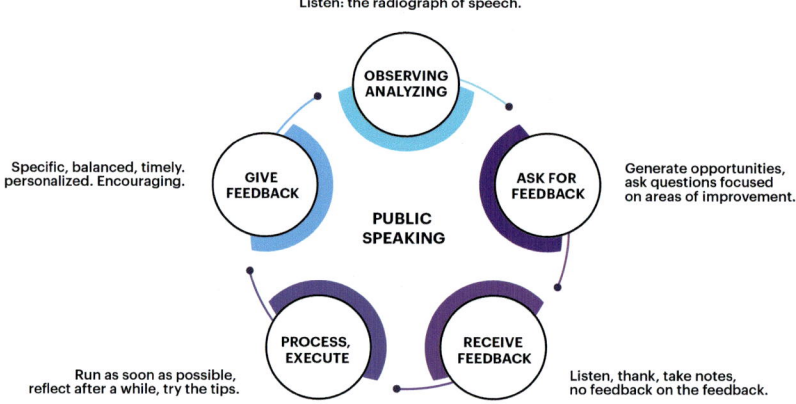

PS: if you have feedback on this chapter, I would love to hear it, read it, talk about it[4].

---

4 I'm a LinkedIn post away (Isabella Valassidis)

Isabella Valassidis

An expert in strategic communication with over a decade of experience advising professionals,
managers and entrepreneurs.
Master in Management of Communication Companies from the
University of Navarra, has dedicated his career to show how communication drives personal and
professional growth.

Currently she is a Public Speaking Coach at IESE Business School and
dedicated to communication management in the education sector.